WO

Farrukh Dhondy is a screenwriter, playwright and bestselling novelist.

Born in Pune, India, in 1944 he went to school and college in Pune and then to Pembroke College, Cambridge. He graduated in 1967 having read Natural Sciences and English. He went on to do a thesis on Rudyard Kipling at Leicester University and then taught in London schools.

He began his writing career while earning a living as a teacher and wrote books, TV dramas and stage plays. In 1983, he was appointed to an executive position in Channel 4 TV.

In his incarnation as commissioning editor for multi-cultural programming for Channel 4 (1984–97), Farrukh commissioned hundreds of hours of TV in all genres, including the Oscar-nominated *Salaam Bombay*, Shekhar Kapoor's *Bandit Queen*, and award-winning TV shows like *Desmond's* and *Family Pride*.

WORDS

From Here There and Everywhere or
My Private Babel

FARRUKH DHONDY

HarperCollins *Publishers* India

First published in India in 2015 by
HarperCollins *Publishers* India

Copyright © Farrukh Dhondy 2015

P-ISBN: 978-93-5136-490-0
E-ISBN: 978-93-5136-491-7

2 4 6 8 10 9 7 5 3 1

Farrukh Dhondy asserts the moral right
to be identified as the author of this work.

HarperCollins *Publishers*
A-75, Sector 57, Noida, Uttar Pradesh 201301, India
1 London Bridge Street, London, SE1 9GF, United Kingdom
Hazelton Lanes, 55 Avenue Road, Suite 2900, Toronto, Ontario M5R 3L2
and 1995 Markham Road, Scarborough, Ontario M1B 5M8, Canada
25 Ryde Road, Pymble, Sydney, NSW 2073, Australia
195 Broadway, New York, NY 10007, USA

Typeset in 11.5/14.5 Garamond by
R. Ajith Kumar

Printed and bound at
Thomson Press (India) Ltd

CONTENTS

INTRODUCTION

This ramble through words and phrases that arise from the interaction of different languages and cultures is decidedly not, and was never intended to be, *Hobson-Jobson* – the dictionary of Anglo-Indian or Indo-British words and phrases, compiled lovingly and painstakingly by Henry Yule and Arthur C. Burnell in 1886.

Long before I knew that *Hobson-Jobson* was the title of their compilation, I had heard my grandmother use the phrase. She pronounced it 'owhson-jhowson', and used it to mean a noisy gathering of people. For instance, if a collection of relatives from Mumbai (then Bombay) was expected to descend upon our household in Pune (then Poona), she would say, in Gujarati, 'I have to get to the market and stock up on chapatti flour before the owhson-jhowson arrives.'

From Yule and Burnell, I learnt that the term 'hobson-jobson' derives from Shia Muslim Moharram processions, in which people mourn the death of their martyrs, Hassan and Hussein, by walking through the streets beating their chests and crying, 'Ya Hassan! Ya Hussein!' The cry was progressively perverted to 'hobson-jobson', and came to mean a noisy gathering.

In my time in Pune, there was a Shia Muslim mosque and a settlement of houses a little distance from our neighbourhood called the Haji Mohammed Javed Isphani Imambara Buildings. The name of the 'colony' – which is what Indians call a collection of houses which would, in Britain, be called an 'estate' – proclaimed itself in green lettering on a concrete arch at the entrance to the compound. From under the arch, on a particular Moharram night, a procession of believers would emerge and walk down the streets. The women would beat their chests and the men would lacerate their backs with metal blades tied to whips in acts of penance. My grandmother no doubt picked up the term as perverted by the English transference, and made no connection with the Islamic rite. If she had made the connection, she would probably never have used the phrase.

I am not up to the task of compiling a dictionary of Indo-Brit and Anglo-Indian words. I will confess that this is a somewhat random collection of words and phrases that intrigue me. It deviates from the Hob-Job endeavour, and achievement, by including words that have nothing to do with the Indo-English context but are, for instance, common Hindustani swear words with folk origins. I have attempted, by questioning the wise, to trace their provenance and meaning.

I have not attempted to define words and phrases definitively either. The anecdotes around them are really all that is unique about this collection. The phrases and words I have chosen are ones that have presented themselves to me in speech or writing, ones with origins I have wondered about because they are very commonly used and their etymology rarely discussed, or because of the contexts in which they presented themselves to me.

Some of the words are rude, but the sensitive can skip these, though they were probably the most difficult to penetrate or get to the bottom of, so to speak.

WHEN IS A DUCK NOT A DUCK?

During my teenage years in Pune, in the late '50s and '60s, the invasion of American culture had begun in earnest. My friends and I bought and read MAD magazine assiduously. There was a regular cartoon feature in which crowds gathering in a street would cry to each other in speech balloons, 'Is it a bird? Is it a plane?' The chorused answer would be, 'No, it's Superman!'

We improvised a parallel. When Bombay duck was served up at a meal, someone would inevitably ask, 'Is it a bomb? Is it a duck? No! It's stinking fish!' Which was as useful a clarification as one needed to tackle it on the plate – but it wasn't strictly true. A Bombay duck is not a fish; it's an eel. Its habitat is the Indian Ocean. It acquired its name through a frequent, almost universal misspelling. Restaurants in India will spell it as such on the menu and place the item under 'fish', which inevitably makes people wonder why a variety of duck is not with the other poultry.

Anyone who has visited Bombay – or, indeed, the western coastal cities of the Indian peninsula, such as Goa – may have noticed the all-pervasive smell of drying fish. The fisher folk hang them on strings like washing, or lay them on mats on beaches and rocks to dry in the sun. It's an acquired taste in odours. I grew up with it and don't find it offensive in any way, but perfectly understand why the unaccustomed do. So how did an eel get to be called a duck? Dried by fishermen of the west coast for preservation, this marine food is served in various delicious preparations, from Parsi sweet and sour 'patio' to Goan pickles and Maharashtrian spiced and dry-fried 'bombil' – the local name for Bombay duck.

This product or delicacy of the coasts was no doubt sent to inland markets and consumers, up the steep Western Ghats, presumably on donkeys or mules and thence by bullock carts. That is, until the British Raj in the 1840s began to build railways to take and fetch their trade inland from ports such as Bombay, Calcutta and Madras. Part of the inland-bound cargo was the dried eel, almost a staple food for the population of the Bombay hinterland. The railway bogeys carrying this cargo by the ton must have exuded a rather strong odour.

The British officials who ran the railways from the 1840s would not deign to identify the cargo of the redolent wagons as 'stinking fish'. They euphemistically labelled it 'Bombay dak', dak being the Hindustani word for the travelling post. Hence also 'Dak bungalow', the rest houses in which the carriers of mail, or despatches before the railways were established, would pass a night on their travels. The spelling, through some process analogous to what children might call 'Chinese whispers', or through non-railway Englishmen not knowing or acknowledging the word 'dak', got transformed to 'duck', and so it stayed and came down to us.

Quite apart from the etymology of the word, a fact I found of some interest was that Sigmund Freud's first research paper was not on any psychological subject, but on research and dissections he had conducted on the sexual organs of eels. He was looking for their testicles. So when next you see, shall we say, a Parsi gentleman fiddling with the Bombay duck on his plate, it's possible he would be continuing or consolidating Freud's research.

A COUNTRY FOR A LIME

Anyone who eats Indian food, including every Indian, should at least pause at the fact that before the Portuguese and British began to trade with India and colonized little bits of it, there were no chillies or potatoes in the subcontinent.

Just as Walter Raleigh brought potatoes and tobacco to Europe, and thence to India, the Portuguese brought varieties of chilli from their South American adventures and conquests to India as late as the fifteenth or sixteenth century. North Indians called the new ground vegetable, the potato, an 'aloo' – an Urdu derivation from Arabic. In western India, the English word was perverted into 'batata'.

Of course, there were spices galore in India and these were what colonial powers including Britain, France, Portugal, Denmark and Sweden came in search of. Still, it's odd to think of Indian cuisine without the sting of chillies. Stranger still to think that, had it not been for the initial trade which led to the colonization of India, the curry house staple dish of spicy potatoes, 'Bombay aloo', would not exist.

———

The mango, in its 3000 varieties, is native to India. Though one can buy Indian mangoes in most South Asian immigrant enclaves in Britain, some fruits one takes for granted in India haven't reached European shores or markets in noticeable numbers.

One of these Indian fruits is the mosambi. It's a yellow-skinned delicious citric fruit, as sweet as the sweetest orange, but not as sour or large as a grapefruit. It's freshly squeezed juice is available in restaurants, at juice-stalls and on the roadside in most cities.

English-speaking Indians and English-menued establishments have taken to calling the mosambi 'sweet-lime'. This has become its 'English' name, and that's how it's referred to, sold and advertised – as though it is a recognized English fruit. It's a perfectly appropriate label as it is sweet and it does turn, as does a lime, from a raw green skin to a ripened yellow. It's much larger than a lime, but then we are told, size doesn't matter.

There was, however, no need for such an invented name. The word 'mosambi' is an Indian corruption of the English description of the fruit, which the Portuguese colonialists introduced to India, bringing it in from their eastern territory in Africa. The description was 'Mozambique orange' and was soon popularized all over India as the mosambi.

BREAD ALONE

The bakery in the street called 'Gauli Wada', the street of the cowsheds, a few hundred yards and a bend from my home in Pune, was run by a Goan family. They called it Barko's Bakery. I would be sent out in the late evening by my aunts for a fresh loaf for the morning's breakfast.

Our cook, Hukam Ali, referred generically to the chappatis, parathas or naans that he made, as 'roti'. These were the pre-colonial traditional ways of turning wheat into bread, though naan, with its inflating yeast content, was brought from central Asia and Persia by the Mughals in the sixteenth century.

The loaves of bread bought from Barko's were called 'double- roti'. I've never got to the historical or etymological root of this particular multiplication – why double? Perhaps because the yeast and dough mixture was kneaded twice or perhaps because the loaves were taller than the most puffed-up naan.

Hukam Ali bore no ill will to this rival roti. He would, on occasion, stop by to buy some himself and I witnessed him dipping slices of it in his tea. There was no nationalistic preference in our household – as there was in some high-caste Hindu households – for traditional Indian bread. Some families never ate double-roti or even the Muslim-associated naan. It was always chappatis or the thicker, oiled parathas.

We ate double-roti for breakfast and traditional rotli – the Gujarati variation of roti – for dinner. In our Parsi household, it was strictly rice in the afternoon and wheat at night. The bought-in loaves at breakfast were eaten with butter and jam or toasted. Each category of bread had its province. The chappatis were kept wrapped in a muslin cloth in the kitchen on a plate or in the 'meat-safe' – a wooden-framed cabinet on legs with wire-mesh walls and door. The double-roti loaf was consigned to a tin, a bread-bin on the dining room sideboard, beside a serrated bread-knife and round, tapered breadboard.

Loaves of bread were either known as double-roti or as 'paoon-roti', abbreviated to 'paoon'. Shaped as discrete crusty buns, the same bread was, and still is, known as 'broon paoon'. The 'broon' probably being an Indian rendition of 'brown'.

It was our cook Hukam Ali who explained to me the origin of the name 'paoon' for these yeast-treated western loaves of bread. Chappatis, parathas and fried puris did without fermentation and risen dough. Hukam Ali told me that the dough for paoon – flour, water and yeast – was made not in domestic but commercial quantities. The large quantity of dough was impossible to knead by hand. These communal, or even industrial quantities, unlike the amounts we kneaded for rotis in our households, were mixed and then pounded and kneaded by foot or even several pairs of feet. And the word for feet in colloquial Hindustani, on the west coast of India where the Portuguese set up their colonial enterprise, is 'paoon'. Thus, paoon-roti, foot-bread became simply 'paoon'.

Hukam Ali's etymological explanation conjured up visions of the Goan Barko family in shorts or folded-up trouser legs or short dresses or skirts, pounding yeasted dough in a vast tray by dancing on it. Had I at the time seen a film (there was no TV in India then) of Italians pounding grapes to pulp and juice to make wine, or had I read about such a process and formed some mental image of it?

INVENTION FALLS FLAT

Even the most chauvinistic Italian would accept that the constraining of wheat flour into strips or hollow cylindrical strands to be boiled and served with several dressings as tangled pasta, was a technique brought by their renowned traveller, Marco Polo, from his sojourn in China.

There is no doubt that long before Marco Polo, wheat, in all its glorious capabilities was part of the staple of Italy's cuisine. But when the famous Venetian returned with his recipes, he introduced the stringy versions. The Chinese noodle then evolved into various famous species becoming spaghetti, vermicelli, macaroni and other subtle variants.

The lesser known adventures and discoveries of the same Marco Polo are those of his journey through India. On his way back from China in 1292, Marco landed with his 300 companions on the Coromandel Coast of India. He records his experiences and observations in his book called *The Travels*.

In this log of his experiences in India, he talks about the humility of the court and the king of Coromandel, who eschewed thrones to sit on the ground. Having been born of earth, he said, he would humbly stay close to it. He records the fact that the populace of India, Hindus in all likelihood as the Muslim conquests of the northern part of the subcontinent had not penetrated south to the Coromandel, ate with their right hands and reserved their left for less savoury bodily performances.

He writes about eating and feasting in the Coromandel kingdom but doesn't record any recipes or tell us how the food was cooked. He returns to Italy via the Malabar Coast.

It is historically recorded that several years after his return to Venice, pasta as we know it, began to be generated in Italy.

Marco and his crew brought their innovations from abroad and some have been cheerfully adopted. One of these innovations is a flat, yeasted bread, sometimes made in the shape of a slipper. The Italians today call it 'slipper bread' or ciabatta. Though the bread only came into commercial prominence in the 1980s, it must have been known to Italian cuisine since at least the return of Marco Polo.

Of course, it's not a proven or even provable historic fact, but isn't the slipper shape the same as that of the tandoori naan? And isn't the name ciabatta somewhat similar to chappati, which Marco may have noted was the Indian staple from wheat?

RANKING

When one hears the phrase 'big cheese' in regular use in Britain, one imagines a character out of Lewis Carrol enthroned and with the insignia of pompous superiority. Does he have a face like the man-in-the-moon?

The phrase is used to indicate that the person being discussed is the grand panjandrum himself or herself, a power in the land or, indeed, the 'top-dog' in the institutional hierarchy.

This canine description, 'top-dog', carries with it the connotation of having fought the other dogs for the position and won their respect through superiority of force.

Kipling's Akela, the top-dog of the wolf pack in his Jungle Books, is called the Lone Wolf. Kipling doesn't tell us that he acquired this position of alpha through brute force and successive combat. It was more through age and wisdom. The very title, 'Akela', demonstrates Kipling's conviction that the apex is a lonely place and that the leader keeps his own counsel.

No such aloofness of power clings to the idea of being a big cheese. That sounds a roly-poly leadership, especially if one thinks of cheese wheels as large as commercial French ones or the great cylinders of Cheddar one sees in English farmers' markets.

Somehow the users of the phrase haven't in recent times wondered, (or wondered aloud in my hearing), how a cheese came to be a metaphor for grandeur. Cheeses are traditional humble smelly things, fit to fill sandwiches, grate onto pasta or bait rat-traps.

However, to speakers of Hindustani, the phrase 'big cheese', born in the days of British colonialism in India would be spelt 'big cheez'. Nothing to do with dairy products. 'Cheez', being the word for 'thing', the phrase was used to mean the big thing itself, the eminence, the object at the top of the pile.

The same Hindustani speaker will recognize phrases such as '*woh toh bahut badi cheez hai*' or '*woh khud ko bahut badi cheez samajthey hain*', the first acknowledging a pre-eminence and the second remarking on the conceit of one who believes him or herself to be superior.

I knew a gentleman called Akumal who conducted a trade in art objects. It's a tricky and uncertain business, much like betting on the horses. But when he pulled a coup of any financial sort he would ask for one's acknowledgement and the accompanying acclaim with a sly smile and jiggling eyebrows by saying, 'Akumal kya cheez hein?' – 'What a thing of wonder is Akumal.'

And of course the young man or woman who is known to have adventurous sexual mores is known as a chaloo cheez, literally 'a moving thing', but with the connotation of knowing or conniving. Verdi's librettist in *Rigoletto* tells us that la donna è mobile, or that women are 'chaloo cheezes', and he uses the same idea of mobility for fickleness.

Incidentally, I have asked several Americans, citizens and denizens of the country from where the adjective originated, what exactly 'cheesy' means. It's quite the opposite of 'big-cheesy' if there ever was such a phrase. To get down to brass tacks, it means something undesirable or in bad taste or even something that exudes a metaphorical discomforting smell.

And those brass tacks? How did that phrase get to mean getting down to the bare truth? Perhaps it has something to do with wearing away unnecessary or disguising layers and veneers till the mechanism of the fix is revealed.

SIGHTINGS

I used to teach in a school in a very working-class area of London. The white cockney kids were quite taken by gadgets, designer objects and pornographic pictures and did a brisk trade in all those and in other fads. The word they would use in a request for examining something, having a look at it, was 'butchers' as in, 'Gi'ss a butcher's!', which in standard English would be rendered, 'Give us a butchers', and would in namby-pamby English be rendered as 'May I be permitted to have a peep?'

The idiom had to be explained to me. Cockneys are very proud of using what is known as rhyming slang, where the word you want to convey is rendered as the word which accompanies one which rhymes with the target word in a well-known phrase.

This may sound convoluted, but examples will make it clear: instead of saying 'wife' you substitute the word 'trouble' because the last word of the phrase 'trouble and strife' rhymes with 'wife'. Or if one wants to say 'stairs' you may say 'apples' as it associates with 'apples and pears', the last word of which rhymes with 'stairs'.

There are standard cockney rhymes and the origins of some have been obscured by time. If one wants to say someone is talking nonsense or 'balls', you can say, 'He was talking a lot of cobbler's' and that comes from 'Cobbler's awls' – the second word rhyming with balls.

The frequently used one, which was used in the title of a Carry On film and which is derived from colonial Raj lingo is the word 'Khyber' derived from Khyber Pass, with Khyber used to substitute for 'arse'. The British genre comedy film was called *Carry On Up The Khyber* and the British army phrase was 'shove that up your Khyber'.

One of the most curious ones I overheard, and probably not standard usage as I only encountered it once in a pub, was a gentleman asking the barman for a 'Vera and Phil'. The barman understood what was required and mixed the punter a gin and tonic. I worked it out with a little help from the others at the bar: Vera Lynn to mean Gin, and Philharmonic for tonic.

The slang is used euphemistically to soften outright vulgarity. I have heard very many ladies use the word 'berk' for a person they dislike, using it as one would, in American argot the word 'jerk'. The word's cockney slang derivation is rather more rude. It is a shortening of the phrase 'Berkley hunt', which I presume was a famous hunt in Berkshire. In the rhyming slang it means the 'C' word describing the female genitalia which rhymes with 'hunt'.

The word which is not derived from cockney slang, with the same meaning as 'butchers', meaning a glimpse or a look, is 'decker'. So one may, and does, say, 'Let's have a decker', which doesn't mean a double-decker London bus. It means, 'May I

have a look?'. The word 'decker' comes from the Hindustani
'dekho', which means 'look!' used as an imperative.

The word was carried back to England by returning soldiers
or, indeed, administrators, though I haven't come across it in
upper-class prose or in British stories about India. It remains
common usage and most British people will know what it
means, though they may not use it themselves.

It isn't used the same way in Indian English. The distortion
from 'dekho' to 'dekker' is entirely English. In Indian
usage it would be 'let's have a dekho', using the Hindustani
pronunciation in an English sentence.

ENDEARMENTS

We Parsis have been traditionally lampooned and caricatured as willing tools of British colonialists. I can't say I recognize the description as universal. My granduncle, Rustomji Dhondy, my grandfather's brother, was a staunch anti-imperialist for all his adult life and followed and adopted Gandhiji's precepts. I lived in his house in Mumbai for a year as a teenager and had to learn (or endure) his ways and was subjected to his nationalistic politics. He was a strict vegetarian, only wore khadi and wouldn't wear leather shoes or slippers but went for those made of cloth or hemp or plastic. There were no photographs of any king or queen of Britain. The only garlanded portrait was that of Mahatma Gandhi and there were ungarlanded ones in black and white of his ancestors and mine.

Nevertheless, I did, especially as a child, come across Parsi households with portraits of King George V or even Queen Victoria. I can't remember anyone uttering paeans to these monarchs or pledging their allegiance to them, but very recently I had a rather embarrassing and amusing experience.

At a Mumbai literary conference in 2008, I was asked by

some writers I knew from the UK to take them out for a meal, since I had grown up in and was acquainted with Bombay and its best eateries. They wanted to get away from the party meals catered for by five-star hotels. I said I'd take them to The Britannia to eat a Parsi meal.

The café was just about to shut down, but I spoke to the proprietor in Gujarati and bribed the cook to stay and we were given a table, the only clients that late afternoon. We ordered what I recommended as typically and exclusively Parsi, and as we ate our meal, the aged Eminence Gris of the establishment, probably the grandfather of the current manager, came down the steps from some inner chamber wearing a Parsi prayer cap and carrying a photograph album.

He had spotted the Britishers and was eager to show them the pictures of Prince William and Kate Middleton he had collected. One of our company was an eminent novelist to whom he turned and asked, 'Do you know Elizabeth?'

She said she knew several women of that name. He qualified his initial question by saying he meant Queen Elizabeth the Second. The company confessed they were not personally acquainted with Her Majesty. He was undeterred. He said on behalf of the people of India he wanted it conveyed to her that the British Raj should return to the subcontinent as self-government and democracy in India were failures, and the days when the British ruled were more settled and happier.

I assured the company that the reverend gentleman was entitled to his view, but it wasn't that of the mass of Indians or, indeed, of more than a few very eccentric Parsis. I am not sure I convinced them.

It is of course true that the Parsis, a prosperous peasantry in Gujarat from the time they migrated to India from Iran in the eighth and ninth centuries, became urbanized under British colonialism and patronage by becoming suppliers and traders of all sorts in the wake of European enterprise in India.

The canard that the Parsis attempted to be pseudo Europeans may have had a pinch of truth in it. But only a tiny pinch, the dose of salt that flavours the canard. I never knew more than a handful of anglicized members of my community and those were mocked as caricatures.

Nevertheless, Parsis did adopt some culinary habits from the British and some words and phrases derived from English, which seem to be the preserve of the community.

One of the phrases commonly used for attractive women by Parsi friends and acquaintances was 'mailaan-o', the 'o' denoting the plural. So one might say 'I'm going to the races tomorrow to bet on the horses and appreciate the mailaan-o' or 'How was the wedding? Lots of gorgeous mailaan-o?' I thought the word was Gujarati or, at worst, Gujarati slang. It isn't. It's a corruption of what Parsis heard the British sahibs call their memsahibs when they addressed them as 'my love'!

APPROVALS

As in any language or culture, there are terms of approval with fairly obscure origins. The current usage in rude England to express approval of anything is, 'It's the dog's bollocks!' It's not the sort of phrase that would be used in gentlemen's clubs in Pall Mall, but one would certainly hear it amongst football fans on the stadium terraces or overhear it in an English pub.

A friend with no pretensions to class recently told me that he had been to the newly opened Bangladeshi restaurant located near a pub we frequent.

'What's the food like?' I asked.

'It's the fucking dog's bollocks,' he said. There would have been no higher recommendation. In literal terms, it would be nonsense. Why the testicles of a mating dog should connote perfection in a chicken tikka masala – or whatever my friend chose from the rich menu of the Star of Bengal – will have to remain a mystery.

I have noticed, on occasion, that the testicles of some dogs are shiny and almost glowing. It's not something I am proud of having noticed, but the truth will out! I suppose the originator of the phrase might have done the same and perhaps the maxim 'all that glisters is not gold' crossed his mind and he thought such a lowly object could indeed be an icon of excellence.

———

I don't know where 'bees knees' comes from either, but as a term of approval it is probably a playful corruption of the word 'business'. The term 'getting down to business' does mean getting things done. The hairy knees of the insect as seen through a microscope, have, unlike the dog's bollocks, nothing to recommend them as symbols of approval. They are not shiny, and if one were the size of a microbe, would probably appear to be a forbidding forest.

Then, as terms of superiority or approval go, there's 'the cat's whiskers' which carries a connotation of pomposity or pride. One can see that it may be the principle adornment of feline features, though tigers' pupils burning bright and the tribal markings on some creatures belonging to the cat family are also striking.

———

In my teenage years, the most popular phrase used to express the triumphant conclusion to a task or the crushing of an opponent was 'maar diya papadwaaleh ney!' It literally means that the papad-maker has scored a hit, though why this trade is associated with victory remains a mystery. A phrase I later heard, more prevalent in northern India than in my days in Pune, was 'good man the lalten'. It was unquestioningly used as a compliment, a term of approval or of appreciation for a task well-accomplished. The 'good man' was the intelligible part and I always assumed that the 'lalten' was added to give the phrase a musical cadenced balance. Or did it mean a red colour as the word 'lal' means red and is used as an endearment? Not so. The 'lalten', I discovered, was an Indian corruption of 'lantern'. It was appended to 'good man' because the phrase came ready-made to India through the import of lanterns made for the Indian railways in the middle nineteenth century by a firm in England, probably Birmingham, called Goodmans.

The Goodman lantern had a patented grip and was, of course, enclosed in a metal frame and, behind its double panes of glass, was a secure lantern very much less likely to cause burns or set off a fire. On occasion the phrase is extended: 'good man the lalten, bad man the diya!'. This refers to the naked flame of the terracotta lamps used in houses being relatively unsafe.

FUEL

One of Kipling's short stories takes a nineteenth-century Indian to London where he marvels at the trains running underground and the streetlights running not on oil, but on gas.

In India, use of gas in cylinders, small or large, or through the mains to supply household fuel for cooking, is a recent innovation. Even in my childhood, all the cooking in my grandfather's house was done on wood and coal stoves, though there were Primus stoves on which lighter cooking such as breakfast could be undertaken. These stoves were fuelled by kerosene, which was pumped to turn it through pressure into a gas that was then lit in a metal mantle in the centre of the grill on which the cooking utensil was placed. The same principle of pumping liquid kerosene to pressure it into a gas mantle was used in lamps and, in the youth of my parents' generation, in street lighting.

The fuel used was kerosene, described in India as 'mitti ka teyl', which literally means 'oil of the earth'.

Another generally used word is 'ghasleyt', a direct perversion of 'gas-light', which when first introduced by the

British was fuelled by kerosene and not by gas at all. The idea of gas light may have come to India with the Primus stove. The kitchen-annexe of the dining room in my aunts' house in Pune had two sorts of stoves. One was a Primus and the other, a Criterion. The Criterion has a cotton wick which was dipped in the kerosene reservoir and burnt the oil directly. The Primus had a manually operated pump in the kerosene reservoir and when activated with vigorous strokes converted the oil into vapour, which then emerged from a mantle and was lit.

IRANI CAFÉ TALK

We Indians often call a restaurant or café a 'ho-tle'. There were many such in Poona where I grew up. The ones in the cantonment and near the railway station – where we as college students would, taking a break from cramming chemistry equations or battling problems of integral calculus, go for a cup of tea at two in the morning – were mostly 'Irani restaurants'.

There evolved a language of service in these cafés, which was an amalgam of transformed Hindustani and English. Half-a-cup of brewed tea, the most my friends and I could usually afford, was 'singal cha'. The waiter would shout out the order to the kitchen's serving counter, letting every other client of the café know that the cheapskates had arrived.

On extravagant days, we would order a 'dubbul cha', a brim-full cup.

And if one really had money to spend, we would have a slice of thick bread with butter plastered over it called 'maska slice', the adjective being Marathi for butter.

The cafés advertised their meals of rice and daal and a side vegetable as 'rice plate chaloo ahey' – an amalgam of English and Marathi. I suppose the European equivalent would be 'Pret a Manger'.

When my aunts sent me out to fetch a fizzy drink from one or other cafés at the corner, I would go up to the proprietor at the counter to place the order and he would shout 'lemon batli parsull!' – the batli being colloquial for bottle, and the 'parsull' meaning 'parcel' or as the Americans would have it, 'to go'.

TOWERS BIG AND DIMINISHED

In my college days in the 1960s, the cigarette of choice for 'hard men' who wanted to appear street-wise, to identify with the commonalty or to overdose on nicotine at the cheapest price, was Charminar. Even the packets looked less durable than the brands that gave themselves fancy airs, named New Deluxe Tenor and Navy Cut. The yellow Charminar packets were printed with the picture of the Islamic Monument – one of the popular sights of Hyderabad – with four towers adorning the corners of a pavilion that stands on a thoroughfare with traffic going round it.

The most famous Indian minar is sultan Qutb-ud-din-Aibak's construction. Its location, through the expansion of the city, falls well within the precincts of New Delhi. It is impressively tall and though the guides who badger you when you visit take great pride in its height and scope, it has no discernible function except to proclaim, in the style of Ozymandias, the greatness of the ruler who commanded its construction. Besides this Goliathan totem pole, very little remains to tell of the deeds or doings of Qutb-ud-din.

There is an iron pillar which stands on the same site and

has stood there since the Buddhist-Indian era. The myth attached to this pillar is that the person who can stand with his or her back to it and embrace it with arms outstretched backwards to encircle the pillar till the fingers of both hands touch, shall be the ruler of India.

One wonders whether any aspirant prime minister would deign to undergo the test. I suppose it would not be difficult to get a tribe of long-armed simians who would all qualify to be rulers of the country. Some might say any one of them would do better than some of those India has been blessed with.

It is not known whether Qutb-ud-din knew this story and subjected himself to the test. I like to think he did and, failing it, determined in a rage to build a pillar or a tower so broad at the base that a troop of men holding hands couldn't encircle it. That would put those Buddhist pillars in their place!

The Qutb Minar is never referred to as the 'Qutb Minaret'. English annexed the architectural term 'minar' and, perhaps without any intent to belittle such structures, added the 'et' suffix, making it 'minaret'. The 'et' or 'ette' suffix is normally used to denote a diminished article or object. So, the tobacco product smaller than a cigar is dubbed a cigarette. A laundry that one can house in a small space is called a launderette. So one can only suppose that the Brits left the minar without a suffix out of respect.

This is unique. Minars owe their origin to the need for a tall adjunct to a mosque so that the muezzin's call to prayer can be heard far and wide. The English adoption of the term has added the suffix to all sizes of Muslim towers including the ones that stand at the corners of the Taj Mahal, though they wouldn't call a cathedral's spire a spirette, would they?

MUDDLING THROUGH

The London school at which I taught for several years was called Archbishop Temples. Its headmaster was one W.J.P Aggett who had, in colonial times, been an officer in the British army.

He was a compassionate and pious man with a healthy sense of fun, a determination to keep up with the times and a peculiar way with words, which probably originated from his service in the colonial armies.

The school day, or week, was never without its problems of one sort or another. Mr Aggett would regularly consult with staff members to sort or iron things out. If the problem involved several people and seemed to have ramifications which had to be diplomatically resolved, he would present the situation before describing it as 'a right bugger's muddle'.

If there was any element of pathos, an aggrieved parent or some accident or injury, he would inevitably say 'it has all the elements of Greek tragedy!' If the problem presented a complexity which he asked for advice to solve, he would append any conversation about it with 'this is a regular Horlicks'. We insiders knew what he meant. The particular beverage of malted milk, advertised and used as a perfect sleep-enhancing nightcap, required its powdered form to be thoroughly mixed with water or milk. Mr Aggett used it to mean a mix-up, a muddle resulting from someone stirring things up.

On one occasion he summoned me to his office.

'Now see what our man G. has done,' he remarked. We were alone and he waved a duplicated exam paper at me.

The person to whom he referred, Mr G., was a very rotund, pleasant Afghan gentleman who taught chemistry. He may have been a sound scientist but, despite having lived in Britain for thirty years, married an English lady and raised a family in London, his grasp of written English was not too secure.

'This is a bloody Horlicks, a right bugger's muddle, a regular Ramsammy with all the elements of Greek tragedy. Several parents have complained that their mites couldn't understand the exam paper. Look at question 8. I can't see what he's getting at either!'

I looked at question 8. It said, 'The atmosphere is mad of four pats Nitrogen and one pats Oxygen. How would you profit?'

'What does dear old G. mean?'

'Shall we ask him?'

'This is terribly embarrassing, dear chap. Of course we shall ask him but I thought I'd put it past you first.'

'I think he means that the atmosphere is composed of nitrogen and oxygen in a ratio of 4:1.'

'Yes, I got that, but what does he mean by "How would you profit"?'

'I think he means "How would you prove it?" His chemistry is perfect and his English not so good.'

'Oh dear. Yes, yes. But how do I explain it to the parents. This is a right Ramsammy.'

It was a phrase I had heard him use before but never attempted to analyse or trace. However vaguely, the context provided the clue. It originates in the supposed or actual muddles caused in the paperwork for the British Indian army stationed perhaps in Fort St. George, Madras, now Chennai, by the generically named clerical staff, Ramaswamy. Thence the clerical muddle caused by faltering spelling or syntax – 'the regular ramsammy!'

BUD BUD

The racist tease used to caricature the accents of Indians in Britain is 'bud-bud-bud', spoken rapidly with a rattle of the tongue. It's supposed to be a parodied reproduction of the speech of subcontinentals.

Surprisingly, the first time I heard it wasn't in England and wasn't from the mouth of a white person. My ayah, the nurse and surrogate granny who looked after me in childhood, was a Maratha and would say in Marathi, 'Kashala bud-bud kartos?' which means, 'Why are you prattling on?' It was a word to characterize unnecessary speech.

Whether the parody entered the English language through Marathi must remain a mystery. Though it hasn't become general usage, there is a sort of reverse parody. Hukam Ali, our cook, who sported a fuzzy cap at all times except when he took it off to scratch his balding head, spoke no English. He would parody the accent and speech of the British in conversation or when my friends and I demanded that he do it for a laugh.

He would say, 'Hoi hi, fish fosh, feesh fosh, feesh fosh … yes, no, no, yes, feesh fosh!'

He would hold his features in a grimace to imitate what he thought was the haughty expression of a sahib when speaking.

Years later in Paris, working on a film with the director Jamil Dehlavi, we were staying for a few days in his brother's house. Jamil's brother was, at the time, the Pakistani ambassador to France and occupied the ambassadorial residence in Paris, a grand house which used to belong, they told me, to Sarah Bernhardt.

The household's driver, an unusually short Pathan, was detailed to drive me into the shopping district looking for ink cartridges for the computer printer. We conversed in Urdu as he knew no English. When we stopped three or four times to ask directions, he showed off the smattering of French he could manage.

'Where did you pick up French?' I asked him.

'The embassy sent me to French lessons for months when I first arrived here,' he replied. 'I picked up a bit.'

'That must have been difficult,' I remarked.

'Not really,' he said casually as he stopped to read the road names, 'you just twist your mouth like this when you speak and it becomes French.'

Related to bud bud is 'buk-buk'.

All cultures have expressions to denote a surfeit of words, for going on and on, rambling, for verbal sound and fury which signifies nothing. The English use the phrase 'blah blah'. Americans add the variation 'yackety yak', probably taken from Yiddish. The literary English representation of someone nattering on, is 'rhubarb, rhubarb, rhubarb'.

In the film *The King And I*, Yul Brynner, playing the king of Siam, in most of his conversations, would assume that the words coming at the end of his sentences were redundant and he would conclude with 'et cetera, et cetera, et cetera', taking it to be a Royal English conceit.

Hindustani has thrown up several expressions for meaningless or redundant chatter. One of them is 'buk-buk'. In Marathi it becomes 'bud-bud' as in 'Kashala bud-bud kartos?' or why are you talking nonsense? In Urdu the word for talking rubbish would be 'bukvaas', which retains the 'buk' but sounds grander or at least more elegant than buk-buk.

ROLL ON

The atheistic college friends of my generation found good use for religious processions. We would join the ones that set out at night to the sound of drums, carrying statues of Ganesh, for example, if it was a Hindu procession. If it was a Muslim feast, the processions carried 'taboots' or 'tajias', towering reproductions of the Kaaba, constructed using bamboo frames to make large scaffoldings covered with silver paper of various colours. A score or more men would carry or drag these around the city before drowning the modelled towers in the river at dawn. The town's municipality would facilitate the passing of the Moharram processions by levering and lifting the overhead electric wires at road junctions to allow the towers to pass under them.

We didn't join in either of these festivities with any religious intent as the thousands of devotees and the devout did. It was, for us – be it the Hindu festival of Ganesh (known in Pune as Ganpathy) or the Moharram Muslim gathering – an opportunity to stay out in crowds through the night, to smoke 'ganja', cannabis in its dried-leaf form, and dance in the streets to the unceasing drums.

———

The procession in Orissa that celebrates the form of the God Vishnu in his incarnation as Krishna sets out from the temple in Puri named after Jagannath, one of the names of the incarnation. The chariots carrying the idols or images of Krishna, Subhadra his wife and Bala his elder brother, are fitted with wheels and axles of stone. The legend says that these huge chariots rumbled through the streets, crushing devotees in their path. The Jagannath chariot thus gives its name to a gigantic and unstoppable force, a 'juggernaut'. The word is literally applied to a large vehicle or, metaphorically, to something, material or abstract, that wreaks destruction in its path.

THE LOOSE SCREW

The British have a few euphemisms for mental disorder. Some of them have been adopted by English speakers in India and some remain peculiarly restricted to Britain and to usage in *English* English.

So if one says, in India, that someone has a screw loose and especially if the phrase is accompanied by the gesture of a forefinger applied to the side of the forehead and twisted this way and that, it would be understood as a sign of craziness. In fact, the phrase has been widely used in demotic Hindustani translation as in 'Woh saale ka screw dheela hein'. With the gratuitous abusive epithet thrown in, it means the subject referred to is not quite right in the head.

The metaphor of the loose screw is derived from the imperfectly working machine.

The association of inadequacy with a mild mental disorder is given literal shape in the 'short of' English idiom. If I want to say that someone is not thinking rationally or not quite there, I would say he's 'one sandwich short of a picnic' or 'one ace short of a pack'. The usage is versatile and allows picturesque invention. So one could say, 'He's a few annas short of a rupee' or 'a few spokes short of a wheel'.

The possibilities, while not endless, are engaging.

A word for mental disorder which has passed into colloquial English through its use by British soldiers in India is 'doolally'. It hasn't passed into Indian usage. The Raj British would use the phrase 'gone doolally' to mean gone crazy and most English speakers in England would recognize it as such. The phrase is sometimes modified, with a finger tapping the forehead, to 'got the doolally tap!'

Perhaps if the phrase had become current in India, its origins would be obvious. The British army, in the later days of the Raj, established a mental hospital for military personnel from all over India in the western Indian town of Deolali. With the tremendous stresses of army life in 'India's sunny clime', as Kipling's poetic narrator calls it, there must have been other wards in military hospitals and other hospitals which specialized in the care of those who are now referred to as 'mentally challenged'. Yet, the institution at Deolali was the main one to which soldiers were referred.

The 'doolally tap', though reminiscent of the gesture of the loose screw in the forehead, had nothing to do with tapping. It was the British perversion of the Hindustani word 'taap', meaning heat, the dreaded climatic cause of delirium.

Though my family has, by the grace of Ahura Mazda, very few connections with mental disorder (yes, I admit this is a matter of opinion), there is a road in Deolali named Dhondy Road, after my family. It was so named in the days of the Raj because the family at that time owned land and houses in that part of the town, requisitioned in large part by the British

Indian army for its own uses. My cousins tell me that the
mental hospital, which still exists, was not built on the land
the family lost to this requisition.

BROTHERS-IN-LAW

In my boyhood or 'laddakpan', to give it its fancy Urdu designation as we are in that sort of territory, I spent my school holidays in Kanpur, or Cawnpore as was, because my army officer dad was posted there.

My mum and dad, being Parsi Zoroastrians, were sought out and welcomed into the small Parsi community of a few hundred souls and some prominent families of that northern town. This community kept up Parsi traditions, getting together for Parsi New Year and other occasions. Some were military folk, some worked as executives in the textile mills which were the principle industry of the city, some were hotel owners and very many were respected professionals – doctors, lawyers, monkey-trappers and the like.

The army and air force personnel came and went. The sons and daughters of the professionals grew up and sought their education and fortunes elsewhere in India.

One permanent Parsi family of Kanpur, acknowledged by the community formally and informally as their senior citizens, were landowners and businessmen called the Jhaveris. The doyen of the clan, old Mr Jhaveri, had a routine of walking at a fixed time in the early evening with a jacket or coat suited to the season, and wielding a walking stick down what was known as 'Maal Road'. The name, in British times, would have been 'The Mall'.

My parents and I, if we happened to be shopping down Maal Road, the main shopping centre above which the Jhaveri clan had a large two-storey mansion, would encounter Mr J. and inevitably stop for a chat. Mr J. was full of very local politics and, as I remember, always commented on this or that building development on the Mall, traffic regulation or some local ordinance that allowed or suppressed the noise of processions – religious and profane.

Now both at that time and later, 'bad words' were strictly forbidden in our household and family, though, as a man of the world, my father must have known that they were all about us. I would never, however, dare to use a swear word in my parents' presence.

Old Mr Jhaveri had no such inhibitions. His favourite epithet, one which was new to me though it was a variation on very standard abuse-usage, was 'beti-chodh' – daughter-fucker! He would punctuate his sentences with the phrase, as American teenagers now do with the meaningless 'like'.

It was a shock to me and perhaps to my parents, though they pretended, out of respect for his presence, not to notice the profanity. I knew the phrase as applied to mothers and sisters, but had never heard it extended to daughters. Perhaps it was north Indian currency not adopted in western India where I lived and went to school.

This incest abuse, applied to males as perpetrators and heaping on them the sin, crime or outrageous monstrosity of having sex with their mothers, sisters or daughters, is peculiar to select cultures. Certainly the Greeks, through the tragedy of the unwitting Oedipus who married his mother, thought it a sin against nature and the gods. Zoroastrian emperors and Egyptian pharaohs, contemporaneous with the Greeks, however, didn't take that view of incest. They married their sisters and perpetuated their clans incestuously so as to preserve the purity of the dynasty that was, they must have believed, divinely destined to rule.

Nevertheless, in most civilizations, a taboo was imposed against incest. Marx and Engels characterized the taboo as part of the feudal arrangements and transactions of land ownership between clans whereby the daughters of the house would be given away in alliances, dowries, bride-price and land trade. Women were commodities or potential wealth.

The British didn't evolve any swear words to characterize incestuous miscreants until the phrase 'mother-fucker' was incorporated into English through the idiom of Black America. That particular usage arose through the taboos born on slave plantations. African slaves were encouraged by the plantation owners to breed and make more slaves without any regard to the institution of monogamous marriage. Slaves were encouraged to procreate regardless of family ties, but within the slave community, the taboo against sex with your mother survived from the African tribal past. Breaking that taboo was a grievous sin and so 'mother-fucker' became a strong term of abuse,

The Indian transgression of decency originates in the sacredness of the mother and the duty of the brother to the sister. These injunctions to respect may well have arisen from the property relations which Marx and Engels write about, but they have long been enshrined in religious texts, belief, ritual and tradition.

———

The word whose sexual connotation is only slyly conveyed is, in its usage, somewhat ambivalent. It's the word 'saala', literally meaning brother-in-law. It is sometimes used as covert insult and abuse and sometimes even as a term of endearment. It crudely means, 'I fucked your sister', even though it literally means, 'I did it with social blessing as I married her'. It can be construed as abuse, but is usually excused as nothing more than uncouth banter.

SHAMPOO

'Teyll, maalish, champi!
Sar jo tera chakraye
Ya dil dooba jaye…'

That's how a popular song from the Hindi film *Pyaasa* goes. The opening words mean: 'Oil, massage, a head massage! If your head spins or you feel your heart sinking…'

Any Indian would know, the street masseur, played by veteran comedian from the 1950s, Badruddin – stage name 'Johnnie Walker' – is offering customers a regenerating head massage with oil.

The process of massaging the head is called 'champi', as in the opening line of the lyric, and is the origin of a word first used in English in the eighteenth century: 'shampoo'.

The connotation of massage has almost disappeared from the Western meaning, except in very ardent saloons, but the idea of cleanliness and, if one is to believe the adverts around the various brands of hair-soap, renewal and regeneration – which our Bollywood song promises – remains.

HOW DO YOU DO?

An old Indian joke, unfairly caricaturing people of a particular religious persuasion, has a gentleman addressed with the greeting, 'How do you do?' answering, 'Both ways'.

I have heard the joke repeated several times and each time the Indian males who heard it immediately understood the meaning. Others and Indian females in the main didn't. The punch line could mean, as the phrase in English goes, that the speaker 'swings both ways' or, in other words, that he is bisexual.

The English, as well as the Indian–English phrase for being bisexual used to be 'AC-DC'. The initials stood for 'Alternating Current' and 'Direct Current', terms from electrical technology which characterized, respectively, the current supplied by a dynamo or generator and that supplied by a battery. Lights on a home circuit ran on AC. Torch lights and the starting mechanism of motor cars, on DC.

The bisexual's dual proclivities were allegorized as a machine that was capable of running on either sort of current. The allegory goes a little beyond saying something like 'he is heads and tails', because AC-DC has the connotation of current or electrical charge which brings to mind stimulation and types of energy – both prerequisites for any form of sexual encounter.

The phrase has gone out of fashion and usage even though I hear it now and then from people of the older (my) generation. The rude words for homosexual people have been replaced by the universal 'gay' and the further distinction of 'gay, lesbian and transsexual' people. The latter phrase, used in politically self-conscious pamphleteering, is somewhat confusing as it mixes categories. 'Gays' refers to male homosexuals, lesbians are the gay females. Why transsexuals, people who have, through surgery, changed sex or simply wish to identify with the opposite gender are classed with gays is not immediately apparent. It may be that all three categories of orientation, preference or preoccupation are subject to prejudices and discrimination.

A discussion I recently had with a woman friend was about the word 'diesel' as used in slang for a gay woman. She insisted that the word originated in the fashion of some lesbian women who wore dungarees, which could be characterized as the uniform of motor mechanics with diesel oil stains on them. She said they should be called 'diesel-dykes' or 'diesels' for short. Plausible, I said, but not convincing. My mind harked back to the old AC-DC divide and I thought the slang originated in a parallel way from an analogy between cars that ran on petrol, the vast majority, and cars that ran on diesel – an alternative but perfectly operational fuel.

MARK OF INNOCENCE

In literature the universal tattoo of guilt derived from the story in the Bible is the Mark of Cain, the mark of the man who kills his brother. If he, after Abel was murdered, was the only man, apart from his father Adam, who was left standing, do we all owe our ancestry to him and carry the sin of that original progenitor with us for all time and through all succeeding generations?

There is no mirror-image mark of innocence arising from Judeo-Christian civilization. Infancy is the age of innocence and all experience, as we grow, is seen as tainting. Innocence gets eroded by experience. As Wordsworth put it:

> ' ...trailing clouds of glory do we come
> From God, who is our home:
> Heaven lies about us in our infancy!
> Shades of the prison-house begin to close
> Upon the growing Boy ...'

In the Indian demotic tradition, the innocence is not lost; it has a distinct origin and takes different forms.

But first a story:

I worked for a UK television channel as a commissioning editor and each week, we had a compulsory review meeting at which we criticized each other's transmitted programmes.

One week, a colleague had screened a programme on the condition of women in Pakistan. In the programme, a middle-aged slum-dwelling woman told the story, in Urdu, of how her husband had brought a younger woman into the house as a second wife and asked her to leave. She said she refused whereupon he gathered some false witnesses and, as the law in Pakistan allows, had her jailed for adultery. She said she returned home after serving her sentence and attacked the new wife, which led to her husband calling the police, gathering more false witnesses and getting her re-arrested. The words she used were '*Phir maaderchod bhonsdi key bhadvey ney moojhe vaapis jail behyja*'. The subtitles on the transmitted film said, 'Then this arsehole sent me back to jail'.

Now, none of my colleagues who were to attend the review meeting understood Urdu. The chief executive of the channel, Michael Grade, spoke to me before the meeting about the programme and asked my opinion. I said it was great but the subtitles missed the richness of the spoken Urdu. He wanted an example.

'The subtitles translated "*maaderchod bhonsdi key bhadvey*" as "arsehole",' I said.

'What would have been the exact translation?' he asked.

'Well, it would have been longwinded and may not have fitted the screen time.'

'Yes, okay, but what's the precise translation?'

'Well, it translates as, "that mother-fucking pimp of a fucked-up cunt sent me back to jail".'

'How wonderful,' he said.

At the review meeting, attended by four female colleagues, he absolutely insisted that I repeat the story and the exact translation as I rendered it.

I did. My rendition was followed by seconds of silence and then our controller of programmes, Liz Forgan, spoke up.

'Do you mean to say, Farrukh, that in Urdu there are distinct words for a fucked-up cunt and a non-fucked-up one.'

'Yes there are,' I said. 'In popular usage, if not in polite usage or in a dictionary, a virginal cunt is called a "chooth" and one that has given birth already is called a "bhonsdi"!'

'How interesting,' she said, and there were grunts of agreement around the room signifying they had learnt something.

The corollary to the story is the origin of the commonly used word, 'choothya'. It is used to mean a fool, an inept idiot. It literally means a person born of a 'chooth', or the first-born, and the culture has concluded that such a person carries the innocence of the virginal vagina with him or her. It's an innocence that experience doesn't erode. Trails of glory indeed!

This isn't the only instance of virginity carrying with it the idea of innocence, though it is probably the only one in which innocence is further characterized as naiveté. Virginity is variously used as a metaphor both in cricket and in nautical idiom. A maiden-over is one in which there is no score, the bowling having resisted all meaningful penetration from the batting. A maiden voyage is a ship's first outing at sea.

A Bloody Mary is a vodka and tomato-juice cocktail with
flavourings, whereas the term 'Virgin Mary' is used as a name
for the same mixture without the corruption of the vodka.

CLOCK-SPEAK

The tradition of the panchayat, the 'council of five', and the panchnama, 'the report of five investigators', being governed by the number five, probably owes its origins to the fact that the Pandavas of the Mahabharata were five brothers and their counsel, which may not have been wiser than that of Krishna or Pitamah Bhishma, was a model for collective decision-making or democracy. I wonder if Sikhism and Guru Gobind Singhji, drawing from Hindu myth, numbered the Panch Pyare, the 'five beloved', after the same tradition.

The decimal system may owe its origins to the fact that humans have five fingers on each hand. Children in every tradition are taught to count using their fingers. Most currencies in the world have moved or are moving towards decimalization, even though for hundreds or even thousands of years one coin contained four of another, as in annas and paisa, and the higher denomination contained sixteen of the lower. So also with the even numbers in the denominations of Sterling. They weren't based on the decimal system or the number of fingers of the human hand. But that changed when the British brought their currency into line with decimalization, with a pound having a hundred pence.

As for weights, the odd system of fourteen pounds making a stone is still very much in use. Weighing machines in millions of British bathrooms, though routinely made in China and calibrated with the complementary system of kilograms, still speak to the populace in stones and pounds. Fourteen seems a strange division for any scale and perhaps the kilogram will eventually prevail.

Furlongs have already disappeared everywhere except in India where someone of whom you ask directions may very likely tell you to proceed for two 'phurlings' in some direction before taking the left turn. Even such measure of distance and the furlong's daddy, the mile, is under assault as the kilometre takes its place.

———

The one universal measure which doesn't seem to have any challenger is the twenty-four-hour clock with its a.m. and p.m. divisions of twelve hours each. The system of twenty-four hours was invented some four thousand years ago in Mesopotamia and adopted by the Egyptians, one of whose Pharaohs was, in 1500 BC, buried with two twelve-hour water clocks.

Though decimalizations of the hours and the clock have been variously suggested, it has as much chance of catching on as Esperanto does of becoming the international language.

The clock face as we know it (before our lit-numbered digital systems) has twelve numbers with the twelve on top, the six at the bottom and an hour hand which points to the principal factor of the time.

The Indian Hindustani lexicon has drawn at least two prominent associations from the image of the clock face. The numbers stand for the position of the hands on the clock face.

One of these is the word 'chhakka'. It has the general meaning of being a person without potency, a useless fellow even though it has a distinct sexual connotation. In literal terms, 'chhakka' means the number 'six'. Only clock imagery explains the derivation. It sees the hour hand pointing vertically downwards at six o'clock. This downward droop is likened to the unerect penis of the chhakka, the ineffectual one.

JUNK

Under the Sangam Bridge in Pune at weekends, there used to spring up, on the vast and rocky river banks, a junk market. It was accessible only by foot and consisted of the stalls of petty merchants under canvas covers propped uncertainly on bamboo poles to protect them and their goods from the sun or from the monsoon rains. The poorer traders had no shelters and just set out their goods on canvas or cloth mats or on wooden crates with no cover.

It was an unclassifiable mela (a fair) and mess of a market. One section sold vegetables and though that wasn't the section my friends and I frequented, it was probably the province of local farmers and sharecroppers selling radishes, onions, potatoes and bunches of coriander from their farms or patches of land. Another part of the market sold canvas raincoats and very rough woollen sweaters, piled in heaps, which potential customers would go through.

What my friends and I were interested in was a particular section of the market which stocked old valve radios and electronic equipment from the pre-transistor era, most of it on olive-green metal chassis and some of it in working order.

There were headphones, transmitters, amplifiers, receivers, walkie-talkies and several fragments of unclassified equipment heaped in piles. The men who were selling this stuff didn't have a clue as to what it was, to what use it could be put or whether it was in good or bad working order. The buyers were rival gangs of college lads, electronic engineering students and eccentric old men who made a hobby of electronics or merely of collecting memorabilia and junk.

Our interest in the market was stimulated by a friend who was something of an electronic wizard. He was studying engineering but his interest was putting together electronic gadgets from spare parts, guided by old editions of an American magazine called *Popular Electronics*.

One of the vendors, who had got to know us fairly well because of the frequency of our visits, took us behind the stall one stormy and very wet monsoon day, and showed us some pistols and rifles he'd acquired and which he was offering us. We suspected it was an illegal deal but one of our gang did buy a pistol with a wooden handle that looked as though it was a prop in a pirate film.

From time to time, canned foodstuffs would appear in this market. They were stored and offered for sale in wooden crates. The foodstuffs ranged from condensed milk tins to canned vegetables and meat. The stuff wasn't selling at all well. There were two inhibiting factors, which warned the public off and kept the customers away though it was going cheap.

One was that the cans had rusted from the outside and were brown-rimmed with their labels, if they ever had any, torn off. The other was the cry of the vendors advertising their goods.

They were shouting 'kundum maal'. I asked one of them what he thought it meant. He said that most of the stuff sold in that market was army surplus, as were the electronics we bought and the raincoats and sweaters that were sold there. 'It's perfectly good stuff. We get it from contractors who have more than they can sell to the military.'

He was wrong. On the sides of the wooden crates in which the cans were packed was one word stencilled on in black paint. It said: 'CONDEMNED'. The boy selling the rusty cans didn't realize that his calling card 'kundum maal' meant, and has passed into usage in India as, 'useless goods' – condemned material.

ENGLAND MY ENGLAND

'There'll be bluebirds over the white cliffs of Dover' goes Vera Lynn's song of the Second World War. It's a nostalgic song about the promised return to England and the line features the sight which today you may spot from the ferry as you approach from Calais – where you may have been to pick up cases of cheaper French wine.

The white cliffs, chalky downs really, may not strike you as the most prominent feature of the land you are approaching, but folk-etymology tells us that it did strike the Latin-speaking mariners of Italy who sailed to Britain before Julius Caesar invaded it. They spoke of Albus, the colour white, and the country whose soil seemed snowy or chalky was named Albion.

In the nineteenth century, Napoleon Bonaparte dubbed Great Britain 'Perfidious Albion'.

Britain has had many names since. Its various nations are England, Scotland, Wales and Ireland and together they are called the United Kingdom or the UK. The different languages of Europe translate the name variously as Angleterre, Gross Britannien and Gran Bretagna. What would one have made in the last century, or the one before it, of a British soldier in India saying he was homesick for 'Blighty'? It wasn't a word used by Indians, except in satirical jest. It means home, England, Scotland, Wales or Ireland. The word comes from the Urdu word, which came to mean 'England', though it didn't start that way.

Edward Lear asks, 'Who or what is the Wali of Swat?' The answer was, and is, that he is the ruler of a kingdom in what is now part of Pakistan. Wali was the word for a ruler and vilayat was the word for his province as a prince can be the ruler of a principality.

In British colonial times, the vilayat was the centre of power from which India was ruled and it began to denote Great Britain. The adjective for anything from vilayat, which meant most manufactured consumer imports of the day, was 'vilayati'. The adjective with the 'i' suffix was then perverted through the usage of the British soldiers in India to 'Blighty', which to them meant Britain.

The word came into literature through the work of Wilfred Owen. It's not there in the colloquial speech of Kipling's soldier characters because it didn't really come into common usage till the First World War.

There were then popular songs which began: *'There's a ship that's bound for Blighty…'* and *'Take me back to dear old Blighty/ Put me on the train to London town…'*

'Vilayat' remains in Hindustani vocabulary as a name for a country which no longer rules India but is forever England. Though, of course, it's not – a Scottish parliamentarian, David Steel, a former leader of the Liberal Democratic Party, once said to me, 'It was actually a Scottish Empire but we astutely blamed it on the English.'

GOING FORTH

One of the dramatic points of the story of the Buddha is his abandonment of the princely life and his family in order to seek enlightenment. In the lore it is known as the 'great going forth'.

One of the saints of the Christian church, the sixteenth-century Lithuanian, St Josaphat, is also supposed to have ventured forth in search of God and, renouncing a life of pleasure and human satisfactions, became a monk. The phrase 'Jumping Josaphat', which expresses surprise or incredulity is probably not derived from the life of this saint. There are several Josaphat's in Hebrew history. According to one version, the name originates with the prediction in the Bible (Joel 3:11) that God will gather the nations of the world in the valley of Jehoshaphat on the day of judgement.

The historian and Indologist A.L. Basham has an alternative etymology for the word. In his study of Buddhism he asserts that 'early Christianity was influenced, directly or indirectly, by Buddhist ideas'. He believe that St Josaphat was so named because he experienced a parallel going forth to that of the

Buddha and the name Josaphat is a Western corruption of the word Bodhisattva.

How likely is this attractive suggestion?

The first time the name crops up in the Old Testament as the name of a warrior king is in the *Book of Chronicles*. Modern scholarship puts the date of composition of *Chronicles* as the fourth century BC, which coincides with the life of the Buddha. Very frustratingly, the same process of dating the biblical compositions concludes that there is no probable date for the *Book of Joel*, so we can't say whether the reference to the Valley of Judgement came before or after the naming of King Josephat.

Basham's assertion would, I expect, elicit the phrase 'jumping Jospehat' from most respectable Hebrew scholars.

REVERSALS

The sound, or names, of the letters 'q', 'y' and 'x' can be phonetically produced by using other letters of the alphabet as pronounced in English: kyoo, wiy and eks do the trick. 'C' can also be written as 'see', but all the others have sounds which can't be rendered without themselves being in the spelling – ay, bee, dee, etc. The name of 'w' can be written as double-u but its sound can't be phonetically mimicked.

The Devnagari alphabet can produce most consonant sounds. There are some exceptions: the sound of 'w', for instance, as we say it in the Roman alphabet with a soft beginning, has no equivalent in Hindi. The closest is the 'v' sound. The phonic sounds of 'f' and 'z' have also been added to the Devnagari alphabet probably because when Urdu evolved these sounds entered the vocabulary. The script could only say 'ph' and 'j', but to turn these into 'f' and 'z' a dot was added above the letter. Hindi can't reproduce some of the values of the versatile vowels of English such as 'a' in 'cat' or 'e' in 'bet'. There endeth the inadequate comparison lesson.

In the local linguistic culture of the school I went to in

Pune, there was a concerted inability among certain boys to reproduce the word 'ask'. They would say 'aks'. One of the more sarcastic teachers would, for the entertainment of the rest of the class in an idle moment, ask one of these stumblers to repeat the sentence, 'I have to ask my brother'. The stumbler would predictably reproduce it as, 'I'll have to aks my bra!' The reply to which would be, 'Why would you axe your bra? Is it too tight?'

It wasn't an attempt to convey the correct pronunciation, just a bit of cruel, if recondite, fun. But such was our school.

This inversion of 'sk' into 'ks' can yield other examples in the verbal culture of the subcontinent. It can't be a dyslexic trait or genetic bias as 'sk' is not an unknown sound in Hindi or Urdu. The commonest usage would be the words for 'whose' – 'Yeh kiski kalam hein' – 'whose pen is this?'. Or the answer: 'Ooski!'

The reverse of 'sk' can also sometimes be heard. Some people pronounce rickshaw as 'rishka'. The lasting inversion of 'k' and 's', one which has passed into history lore and literature, is the mispronunciation of the name of the raider of Persia and the Indian provinces west of the Indus. His Macedonian name was Alexander, known to the worshipful West as Alexander the Great, but to the Zoroastrian descendants of the civilization he desecrated, setting fire to the palaces and libraries of Persepolis and laying waste the cities of the plains, as Alexander the Damned.

To subsequent history in the languages east of the Jordan, he is known as 'Sikander'. The 'X' of Alexander has been inverted into the 'Sik' of his eastern appellation. He goes down in the annals of Arabia and India as 'Sikander'. In some versions, the 'Al' of Alexander, eliminated in Sikander, has been preserved and he is dubbed Al Sikander with distinct Arabian connotations.

A British actor of Pakistani origin once approached me for advice. He said he wanted to adopt the stage name of Al Sikander and wanted to know if I thought it would distinguish him from the mob and bring him fame and fortune. I thought of the consonant inversion that had generated the name and said he ought to be cautious because the mischievous culture of British theatre might render, through a further inversion, Al-Sikander as 'Arse-lickander' and that probably would lead to laughs in casting sessions or in the green room, but not necessarily to fame and fortune.

———

In Kipling's stories (cf. 'In Flood Time') and still in my hearing, Indians render the name of the city Lucknow as 'Nuklao'. Unlike the name Alexander, which is of foreign origin, the city of Lucknow has a very native name. The fourteenth-century Arab traveller Ibn Batuta notes the name of the city as 'Alakhnau'. Legend has it that the city was named after Lakshman, the brother of Ram. Why the Indian tongue should then find it difficult to pronounce remains a mystery. Not all Indians, of course; only those who are influenced by this cultural dyslexia.

———

Another inversion of consonants, owing to the fact that this compound consonant form is not commonly found in Hindi or Urdu, is the use of 'gn'. So very many taxi or rickshaw drivers will call a traffic signal a 'singal'.

BROADCAST

All India Radio was set up by the British and given its English name. The term 'broadcasting' was, by definition, invented after the discovery that radio signals could carry a voice or a sound for miles and miles and then, with shortwave, even round the earth.

The idea of casting, as applied to stones – 'Let he who is without sin cast the first stone' – or to fishing nets, which were cast as widely as possible, applied to voices in theatre. Opera singers and actors are taught to cast their voices to greater distances than the untrained speaker. The idea of casting broadly must have occurred as a 360-degree projection to every angle around a transmitter.

Indian nationalism, while changing the names of central roads in most cities to Mahatma Gandhi Road after Independence, also changed the name of the central broadcasting service to 'Akashvani', the 'serving from the sky'. It's a pretty and inventive, if overly Sanskritized, term. It didn't completely replace All India Radio, a rather staid offering in the genre of the British Broadcasting Corporation. The BBC though doesn't make up a word while the initials of All India Radio cleverly do.

Then TV was invented.

It may have taken some thought to call the new device 'television', but the derivation is literal. Galileo had contributed the word teleskopos to civilization. It enabled him to observe the moon and sun and planets and he quite literally framed the word from tele (far) and skopos (seeing). From telescope to television was something of a leap as it implied a whole new sense. Its inventor, Logi Baird, may have chosen another name such as teleprojection, teleframes or teleview, but those terms don't convey the idea of a whole new human power – as does the 'X-ray vision' which Superman possesses.

TV came to India late. I came abroad for the first time to England in 1964. I had never seen a television set and, having to spend a few days in a boarding house in London before going up to Cambridge, I saw and heard my first goggle box suspended on a shelf in the corner of the dining-room ceiling. It was transmitting a programme called *Top of the Pops*, and the song that I first heard and saw, a great introduction to TV, was Diana Ross and The Supremes singing '*Baby, baby, where did our love go?*' It wasn't like cinema. This stuff was happening in real time. These girls were singing and their song was cast abroad.

When TV came to India it came through the agency of the state falteringly in the '70s and then unstoppably in the '80s with a resultant flowering or flood in the '90s and after.

The state, though dishing out a controlled and bland offering of programmes and government-propaganda news, was imaginative in the name it gave the new service:

Doordarshan. The 'door' was a direct steal from or translation of 'tele', but the 'darshan' was truly inspired as it captures the sense of awe with which one goes before the deity or the guru who has deigned to allow you an audience.

KNOCKED OUT

Indian newspapers are addicted to characterizing institutions by the initials of their names and people by the initials of their office. Each time I am India and reading the papers, I suffer what one may call initialization shock. I can't make head or tail of articles which say, for instance, "The AICC's loan to AJl which was passed by the AGM did not disclose the YI's shares…'

The article from which I quote also says that 'the DC did not give permission to the DLF… and that a CLU was granted… for a SEZ that did not take off'. As clear as Alphabet soup.

Everyone knows what RSS or BJP or PM and CM stand for, but after any period away from Indian politics, I notice a bewildering number of new initialized abbreviations.

In Mumbai in the early twenty-first century there was a spate of attacks on taxi and rickshaw drivers who came from Bihar and Uttar Pradesh to work in the city. I asked who was doing the attacking and was told what sounded to me like 'M&S'. In London one uses this abbreviation for the chain store called Marks and Spencer. I knew that this chain had opened branches in the new shopping malls in Mumbai, but couldn't instantly appreciate why Marks and Spencer would assault or seek to expel Bihari rickshaw drivers. One query later put me right. My informant meant 'MNS' which stands for Maharashtra Navnirman Sena or Sabha, an organization of local regionalist allegiance and a breakaway from the Shiv Sena, which I perhaps would have identified from the initials SS.

What is curious is that the names of organizations and institutions which are in Hindi, Marathi or any other Indian language are rendered in abbreviation using the English alphabet. Hence MNS, RSS, BJP, TMC, SP, UP, BSP and DD for Doordarshan.

In a newsmagazine I was leafing through, there was a curious picture of an elderly man wearing a green shawl and a ridiculously large gold garland. The caption under the picture said BSY launches KJP. Wanting to know what this meant, I read the accompanying article. It said that Bookanakere Siddalingappa Yeddyurappa had launched the Karnataka Janata Party. Perhaps the initials in this instance should be welcome. Or should the august politician be called by a pet name, like 'Boo' or even 'Bo-si-yed' as in the disgraced Chinese politician Bo-si-lai ?

The real translingual abbreviations, getting away from institutional and political initials are the ones invented on our Indian campuses. In my day, a male who seemed to be desperate for sex and wasn't getting any was characterized as 'frusth', short for frustrated. It was incorporated into Hindustani sentences: 'Bada frusth ho gaya'.

The most imaginative of the initialized abbreviations probably arose from Delhi campuses. I didn't hear it in my time in college even though the circumstances which generated the phrase are universal. The phrase incorporates, in very visual terms, the act of sudden frustrations of one's plans, intentions or desires.

'Khade lund pey dhoka', literally 'a deception on an erect penis', is elegant in its crudeness. 'Dhoka', of course, conveys the feel of a physical stroke, a 'down boy!' gesture on the aroused lingam. The phrase itself is used for being led on and then let down and has now overflowed its sexual connotations and boundaries, and I have heard it applied analogously in totally non-sexual contexts.

It is these contexts in which perfectly portly young and old women, who have no idea about the origins of this abbreviation, use it as a phrase. It is applied as a verb for utter defeat and frustration. I once heard a young woman reporting the fact that a rival had wanted to be captain of the univeristy hockey team but, 'She was completely KLPDed!'

DRESSED AS LAMB

'Mutton dressed as lamb' is the catty or undermining expression that the Brits use to describe someone who dresses in the fashion of a younger generation with a view to appearing younger than they are. A mutton and a lamb are, of course, both sheep of different ages, mother and child generation respectively.

The trans-categoric or trans-species phrase is 'wolf in sheep's clothing', but this is only applied to the wickedly intentioned who disguise themselves as innocents.

It was only four decades ago that herds of cattle were still kept and nurtured in the hearts of Indian cities. In Pune, two hundred yards from our street, was a district called 'Gawli Wada', the Cowherds Retreat. One held one's nose as one passed. The herds of cattle were kept in rows of pens adjoining the road, and at particular times in the day would be herded, in a moving army of perhaps fifty beasts, down the road. Traffic would stop till they cleared the crossing. I never knew where the lathi-wielding stalwarts who led and followed them were taking the animals. I was just aware that their function in the city was, in that era, to supply milk by the pail-full to the neighbouring citizens.

The enclosure of the Gawlis was not all stink and nuisance. There emanated from it the sounds of ceremonial music on festive days, and the alleys and houses around the vast cowsheds would be home to wrestling competitions. One stout Parsi gentleman fancied himself as a wrestler and was trained by the cowherds in the wrestling arts. He may have had another surname, but he was universally known as Adi Gawli, 'Adi' being the popular abbreviation for Ardeshir, and 'gawli' meaning cowherd.

The one anomaly of Gawli Wada was that, though it was named after cows, the herd of beasts brought up there were not cows. They were black buffalo, a species common to the west Deccan. The milk they supplied had a faint bluish tinge but I think I drank it in tea or mixed it with my porridge or cornflakes throughout my childhood without classifying it as anything other than cow's milk.

Gawli Wada was erased by the march of progress and high-rise buildings now occupy its space. I didn't imagine at the time that the buffalo that were reared there were bred for slaughter. I thought it was only for their milk. Later of course the unspoken truth emerged and I realized that what was sold and passed off in our town and in the Bombay of the time as 'beef' was, in fact, buffalo meat. I am sure that the beef curries or beef biryanis cooked in my grandmother's house by Muslim or Christian cooks were not 'beef' in the sense of being cows' meat at all.

Which makes me wonder whether the animals reared in the wild west of America, the herds that cowboys in Westerns look after and 'rustle', are actually American buffalo which supply the 'beef-steaks' for which the USA is famous. Which brings one to the hamburgers of fast-food chains. Everyone knows they have nothing to do with 'ham' and are actually beef burgers, but does that mean cow-burgers or buffalo-burgers? What species of animal are those 'doggies' and 'steers' one reads about in the comics?

The universal conversion of meats and confusion of species perpetrated on the English language during British colonial times was the flexible use of the word 'mutton'. British supermarkets today have no respect for the age of the animal – they universally label the meat of sheep as 'lamb' – the creatures who, in Wordsworth's fancy, gambol as to the music of tabors, and in modern cookbooks, make succulent tender cutlets. In India if one is served 'mutton', except perhaps in Kashmir and some recesses of the Himalayas where sheep prosper and are fleeced, it is bound to be goat's meat. Goat in sheep's clothing?

I fancy that the slide of meaning came about as a euphemism on the part of memsahibs. When the colonial sahib asked them what was being served for supper she would reply, 'mutton curry, darling', because the sahib may have been put off by the thought of eating the animals that roamed every street and gutter of the cantonment. But that's a fancy.

Nevertheless, the fact that Indian usage has turned goat into mutton – as wonderful as turning donkey into horse perhaps – is undeniable. Any discussion of the subject with Indian ladies who serve dinners today will assure you that the dictionaries and zoologists are wrong; that mutton is the meat of goats.

One of my favourite eateries in London is the Lahore Kebab House, now something of a restaurant chain. I asked the proprietor if what they served as 'lamb chops', a delicious speciality, were actually goat chops. He assured me they weren't.

Another Parsi culinary delight is what we call 'cutleyss', a minced meat battered croquette of sorts. This is an Indian perversion of the roasted or grilled cutlets of lamb or pork.

SIZE MATTERS

'Give him an inch and he'll take a mile' goes the old saying. The expression doesn't mean that the annexed mile will be passed off to the giver as the length denoted by 'an inch'. It means taking advantage and grabbing a larger portion than was granted or given to you. It would be more cunning to convince the giver that the contract for the inch entailed the surrender of 63,360 inches because he or she had got the denominations of inch and mile mixed up. That would of course mean dealing with a real idiot.

One ought to be precise or meticulous in the matter of measure, just as Portia demanded that Shylock be when he was about to extract a pound of flesh from nearest Antonio's heart. Shylock found it was impossible in this particular operation to be exact and gave up his claim, thus rounding off the plot of one of Shakespeare's most famous plays.

The measure of length occurs again in the phrase to 'half-inch' which is derived from cockney rhyming slang to mean 'pinch', which doesn't mean to take something between the nails of the forefinger and thumb as in 'a pinch of salt' or squeezing someone's flesh as in 'a pinch and a punch for the first of the month!', but it means to steal. It was current in my schooldays though one doesn't hear it as frequently half-a-century or more later.

But some measures have lost their original value. In a Delhi bar once, not wanting to experiment with the extremely variable vintages of Indian wine, and it being a hot day, I asked for a beer. The waiter and my solicitous host asked if I wanted a draught beer or a pint. Used to London measures, I determined I wanted a pint of draught beer and trying to be smart, I said I wanted both.

'Fine,' said my host, and as the waiter who shook his head in assent seemed to understand, my host added, 'Aur merey liye whisky or soda aur barrf alag.'

Indian drinks orders tend to be precise. I suffered from the precision. The waiter returned with the tray with a measure of whisky in a glass, a bottle of soda and a pail of ice for my friend, together with a glass of draught beer with a proud white foaming head and an empty glass which he placed next to a green, labelled half-pint bottle of lager.

'You've brought me two different beers?' I asked.

'That's what you asked for,' my host said. 'I thought you wanted to compare.'

Confusion. Then I remembered I'd said 'both'.

'I just wanted a pint of draught,' I said.

The waiter leaned forward. I think he thought that I didn't know which was which so he stooped to enlighten me.

'This one draught,' he said, picking up the foaming glass gently and putting it down again. 'And this pint!' He touched the half-pint bottle and placed it an inch closer to me.

'That's not a pint, that's a half-pint,' I said

'No, sir, full bottle that is a pint,' he said. 'Shall I pour?'

'The bottle is a half-pint size. Like 37.5 centilitres?'

'This *is* what we call a pint in India,' my host said.

'But it's only half-a-pint. A pint is a precise measure. It's like saying six inches is a foot.'

'Don't know about that, but here this is a pint. Anyway, you got two beers, yaar. By your British calculation a whole pint!'

'That's true. The benefits of misunderstanding.'

I wonder which other measures Indian usage perverts. I have known men measure their bodily part in centimetres and pass them off as inches, obviously under the delusion that size matters. In the measure of alcohol, I think it does.

A MANGO BY ANY OTHER NAME

My Maratha ayah was called Chandri. She was of my grandmother's generation but resisted the more respectful form of 'Chandrabai'. She would accept being called it by strangers whom she acknowledged owed her respect, but to members of the household, she insisted on being called Chandri. It was the name she told my grandmother she wanted to be called when she was first recruited to look after my mother's young sisters.

Throughout her life we got used to her peculiar way of distorting the sounds of English words. Her distortions passed into the household's vocabulary with no accompanying sense of derision. So a shower was a 'saavak' and our Teddy Bears were 'Therybek'.

Chandri would sing us lullabies in Marathi and in her fragmentary Hindi but she had also picked up lullabies, which our grandmother sang in Gujarati and my mother sang in English. Gujarati and Hindi were not so far away in pronunciation from her native rural Marathi, so what she sang, though perhaps she didn't get the full meaning of the lyric, was fairly close to the real thing. English lullabies were a different fettle of kitsch.

The second line of 'Gone to buy a rabbit skin/To wrap my baby bunting in' was rendered by Chandri as, 'Ratna baby bunchheee!'

The rest of the words were variable and were replaced by humming to a very accurately kept tune. Her musical ear was astute enough; it was the syllables and consonants of English that confounded her.

I suppose every language gets lost in transarticulation. In some cases, it takes a certain amount of time and concentration to realize that one word is, in fact, a perversion of the original rather than a freshly coined description.

Chandri's rural Maratha distortions of English were a key to my understanding of how Alphonso, the delicious variety of mango, came to be commonly called 'Hapoos'.

The Alphonso mango is said to be named after Alphonso de Alberquerqe, the Portuguese warrior and admiral who set up a colony on Goa in 1510. Though plausible, it's not true. The mango was named after Nicola Alphonso, a Jesuit monk who took varieties of mango to Brazil and cross-bred them till he came up with this most exquisite of hybrids.

It isn't certain whether the cross-breeding took place in Brazil or in western India, but the presence of the Portuguese in both colonies and their journeying to, from and between them established the hapoos as the aristocratic variety of mango in upper western India, from Goa to Gujarat.

Another Jesuitical cross-breeding resulted in a larger mango with firmer flesh, and it was called the Pereira, after the botanist who bred it. The name Pereira has been lost in time and this variety of mango is known in western India, again through transarticulation, as 'Pahyri'.

NO TALL STOREYS

My father was a civil engineer who had joined the army and become a soldier. If I am asked to characterize his personality, I would say that he was a military man through and through. His mind was devoted to a sense of order and even to the idea that things were, and should be, as authority had commanded them to be. Room for scepticism and questioning was rather squeezed.

Even so, now and then the civil engineer emerged from under the military armour. I remember him explaining to me, in some tedious detail, some features of the houses which, as an army officer family, we lived in. These houses in the cantonments of Pune, Kanpur, Chennai and Cochin were of a particular architectural style, set individually in their compounds with verandas fronted by porches on pseudo-classic pillars.

Dad pointed out the dimensions and function of the ventilators of the sitting and dining rooms, windows near the ceiling through which a bird would occasionally intrude. He talked about Lutyens, the co-designer of the capital of

New Delhi and about a rival architect called Baker. I didn't take it all in.

One fact that did remain was that the single-storey house, the bungalow, was a British invention. For the thousands of years before the British arrived in India, there were dwellings and palaces and pavilions, but this particular style of house, with tiled sloping roofs to allow the monsoon to drain away and often with a wooden frame and pillars, was attributed to the British.

Their first settler intrusion of note was in the south and then the traders' settlement arose in Bengal where the Brits built a trading post with their houses inside a fortification, which was named Fort William. The traders and settlers of the East India Company subsequently, in the latter half of the seventeenth century, after the upheaval of the Civil War and the restoration of the monarchy, acquired the swampy islands which were to become Bombay. The islands were gifted by the Portuguese as a dowry to Charles II of Britain when he married Catherine of Braganza.

The islands were licensed to the East India Company and its officials began to build their houses on the pattern that had proved useful against heat and rain in eastern India. The prototype was the house from Bengal and the native population who constituted the workforce that built them referred to them as Bengal houses or 'banglas'. The British who lived in them rendered the word as 'bungalow'. It has now come to mean any single-storeyed dwelling, but I like to think of it as the neat little thatched or tiled construction with a sloping roof in the midst of thick vegetation – a jungle bungalow.

A ROSE BY ANY OTHER

My parents and uncles couldn't tell me the origin of our family surname. The younger generation tells me that there are 'apps' – whatever these may be – on the Internet, which can trace the origins, antecedents and evolution of any surname. This is, of course, misinformation. I tried, and found that this particular research tool restricts itself to Smith and D'Urberville and the like, and doesn't stretch to Dhondy.

Nevertheless, one can speculate. The surnames of Parsis, who lived a quiet, largely unrecorded life for several hundred years in Gujarat after arriving there as refugees from Muslim oppression in their native Persia, originated in traceable ways. When commerce or necessity of any sort caused Jamshyd, Khurshyd or Ardeshir to travel away from their place of birth or parish, they must have been referred to as the Jamshyd, Khurshyd or Ardeshir from such-and-such place. So names such as Udwadia or Bhavnagri arise from the fact the family originated in Udwada or Bhavnagar. There is a place called Dhond east of Pune, but it is highly unlikely that any branch of our family ever came from, or even ventured, there.

The migration of Parsis began in significant numbers

under early British colonialism, seven, eight or more centuries
after their first arrivals in western India. They moved to
work or pursue a trade, and their surnames announced their
professions. There were descriptions in Indian languages so
we get names such as Mehta, a clerk or accountant, Vakil, a
lawyer and Mistry, a technician or engineer. At some stage
the professions begin to serve in the colonial territories or
contexts and the names change to English: Doctor, Engineer,
Driver and even Captain.

This attachment of profession has led some members
of my family to attempt to trace our name back to a trade.
Dhondy, in the vernacular, means stone-breaker, so perhaps
some ancestor of ours was a mason of sorts. Another
possibility is that he was a convict sentenced to hard labour
– a possibility which we, of course, dismiss.

Then there are the Parsi surnames that are associated with
trades that didn't have distinct professional designations and
had to be constructed by adding 'walla' to the trade or to the
place from which the family originated. So, examples of the
latter would be Poonawalla or Taraporewalla – with a single
or double 'l'.

The wallas of a trade have given rise to the caricatures and
lampooning of Parsis. There are neutral 'wallas', by which I
mean there's nothing intrinsically funny, for example, about
the liquor trader called Toddywalla (more on the word 'Toddy'
later) or Daruwalla. Or, indeed, when a trader in bottles is
called Batliwalla.

The hilarity sets in when a family is called Sodawaterbatliwalla
– a name I have always doubted the existence of. There are
other such dubious constructions: Waysidepetrolstationwalla

and my mythical second cousin twice removed (each time by the police) who now lives in Canada. He is known there as Rustom Immoralearningswalla, having anglicized his original Mumbai name from Russi Bhadva – the word bhadva meaning pimp.

Did I make all that up? Up to a point, yes. What I haven't made up is the maiden surname of my paternal grandmother. She was called Meher Saklatwalla and came from an illustrious family. Her father Jamshed Saklatwalla was a scholar and translator of Rumi and Omar Khayyam from the Persian.

I always assumed that family name originated in a village in Gujarat called Saklat – a perfectly plausible assumption. Not so. One of my distant cousins, a Saklatwalla himself, told me that the name originated in a trade that the family took up. They imported raw jute from Bengal to western India and set up factories to turn it into cloth for making sacks. The trade, an indispensable adjunct to the shipping and packing industries, prospered. Hence, Sack-cloth-wala became Saklatwalla.

———

The Saklatwallas must have made 'gunny sacks' – a term that has travelled into American rural usage. The word 'gunny' comes from the Sanskrit or Hindustani 'goni', meaning crude. The word is out of use but leaves us the English inheritance for a jute bag to carry grain, potatoes, other agricultural products and, filled with sand, to shore up against floods and pile up against bullets from terrorists at check points.

———

Surnames were necessitated in the era of capitalism. In feudal times people were called John O' Gaunt or Richard the Lion Heart. I don't suppose Robin was ever addressed as Mr Hood. The name identified him as the man who wore the monkish cowl. Friar Tuck was so named because the spoonerism of the name (try a fuck) provides a crude folk-tale joke. The craft conglomerates of late feudal and early capitalism bred the Thatchers, Millers and Fishers and, in India, the Watchmakers and Readymoneys.

In south India, people's names are often preceded by their father's name and, before that, the name of their place of birth. So, one of independent India's first ministers was called Krishna Menon, but was always referred to as Vengalil Krishnan Krishna Menon – the first two words being the name of his village and his father's name. This is abbreviated regularly to V.K. Krishna Menon.

Very many Indian surnames are caste names and sub-caste names. Some famous names have arisen in curious ways. The Parsi family called the Petits were so called because their ancestor Sir Dinshaw Maneckji Petit started a textile mill in the nineteenth century and amassed a huge fortune by supplying European firms who were in turn getting rich off the proceeds of trade with both sides in the American civil war.

The family got its name from the French traders who dealt with Sir Dinshaw's father who was of a diminutive size and was dubbed 'le petit Parsi', the little fellow. The name was proudly adopted and the family became the Petits.

Sir Dinshaw's granddaughter Ratanbai, or Rati Petit, married Mohammed Ali Jinnah. Strangely enough, the Jinnah family name also arose from the fact that Mohammed Ali's father was known, because of his small height and frame, as 'Jeenabhai', the tiny one. Mohammed Ali was himself lanky and tall and Rati was reputedly very beautiful and of average stature, but both their surnames arose from a characterization of their ancestors' small size.

Another curious Parsi name, which predates capitalism and naming by profession, originates in the time when Parsis were feudal landlords in Gujarat. They were the Seths, the lords of the manor, and kept a retinue of servants, male and female.

These lords of the manor interacted with their non-Zoroastrian female servants, maintaining some as concubines and fathering their children. These children were not a secret, not even from the Parsi Zoroastrian wife of the Seth and they were given Parsi names though they were brought up, with generous support from their fathers, in the households or quarters of their mothers. In most cases they grew up with their half-brothers and sisters, the offspring of their mothers' husbands. The children of these Morganatic 'marriages', illegitimate in the old-fashioned legal sense, were referred to by their mothers as 'Sethna', the children fathered by the Seth. It was subsequently adopted as a proud surname and its origins forgotten.

The word for heated whisky with water, 'toddy', in current use in Britain as a hot alcoholic and reputedly medicinal drink, originates in the naturally occurring Indian drink 'thadi'. This is the sap of a palm tree, which accumulates in the semi-global bowl at the top of the tree trunk and is a fresh drink, somewhat reminiscent of coconut water, called 'neera'. In its fresh state, taken straight from the tree, it is non-alcoholic, but it ferments rapidly and turns into the alcoholic 'thadi'.

When my grandfather's generation talked of drunkenness on the rural Parsi estates of Gujarat, it was characterized as the demon drink with no medicinal benefits whatsoever.

POLITICALLY INCORRECT

The incorporation of political correctness in verbal usage has become one of the forbidding taboos of language use in the West and, of course, everywhere where the West's sensitivities are imitated. Disabilities, for example, have to be hidden under linguistic euphemism or subterfuge. People aren't fat; they are 'rotundly challenged' or victims who suffer from beer-retention. The word midget is considered rude, and 'vertically challenged', however ludicrous it sounds, has to be substituted.

The sensibility dictating political correctness was born out of kindness and consideration. That it parodies itself in very many circumstances doesn't undercut the original intention or prevalent sensitivity.

'People of colour' is now the preferred term for African-American, which succeeded 'black American', which in turn replaced, through the insistence of black people, the euphemism 'coloured', which was in times past substituted for 'negro' and its offensive derivative. Fashions change and now some people of African descent prefer to be called 'people of colour', and some Asians have adopted the conceit.

So also in India the Dalits insisted on being called 'the oppressed' rather than cover up the political truth with the word 'harijan', the people of God, which Mahatma Gandhi coined and popularized. His motive, now thought of as patronizing, was to get away from the cruel classification of this oppressed section of the population as 'untouchables'.

It strikes me as strange that the Indian chappaterati, the chattering classes which adopt so many intellectual fashions from the West, have not sought to change the terms 'Backward Classes' and 'Other Backward Classes'. These terms are bureaucratically and journalistically abbreviated to BCs and OBCs. The various castes that call themselves 'Dalits' today were, through the considerations thrown up by the Independence movement, offered concessions of advancement in the Constitution of India. These concessions and considerations are listed in the appendices to the Constitution and are known as 'schedules'. The castes and classes named there have acquired the label of 'scheduled castes' and 'scheduled classes'. The irony of the labelling is that the Indian Constitution was framed under the leadership of Dr Ambedkar, himself a Dalit. The castes and tribes have since then been classed, written about and spoken of as 'scheduled castes' or 'scheduled tribes'.

Nowhere else in the world would the adjective 'scheduled' have the same connotation. In the rest of the English speaking world it would mean 'at an appointed or designated time or date'. So 'the scheduled meeting didn't take place' would be an acceptable formulation, but 'the scheduled caste spokespersons handed in their petition' might be a puzzle.

HIGH NOON

In late 2012 history was made at the gates of Buckingham Palace when Jatinderpal Singh Bhullar, a uniformed Sikh guardsman on duty, was allowed to wear a black turban, the insignia of his faith, instead of the regular tall bearskin hat. Bhullar, from the Scots Guards regiment, is also allowed to keep his beard, unlike the rest of the parading ceremonial guards in their uniform of long crimson or blue coats, who are by tradition clean-shaven.

It was in my curiosity-fuelled youth that I asked my father why Sardarjis are offended by the term 'baara bajey' – 'twelve o'clock' – which, on the face of it, doesn't seem capable of giving offence. My dad told me that the canard is founded in the fact that the sun is at its hottest at high noon and that causes covered heads, especially those encased in turbans, to feel the heat acutely and that causes boiled brains and anger.

It seems a plausible enough explanation if one is in Punjab, but now that there is a considerably large Sikh population in Vancouver (is there a settlement in Iceland?) the attribution of annoyance to hot-headedness is less convincing. In

Vancouver's winters and even summers, most people sport some form of headgear.

If one thinks of Guardsman Bhullar, his head at high noon will be considerably cooler than that of his colleagues who wear the tall fuzzy black bearskins.

The heat-oppressed brain theory of Sardarji annoyance always struck me as somewhat childish and suspect. Why would being teased by the shout 'It's twelve o'clock' necessarily result in a connection with hot-headedness and why would generations of Sikhs object vehemently to being called hot-headed in reaction to weather conditions?

So one must, my dear Watson, look for the explanation that isn't elementary. The answer perhaps lies in the first clue.

To annoy a Sikh one doesn't simply shout, 'baara bajey'. The original provocation was, 'Sardarji key baara bajey'.

In some uses, the term 'baara bajey' means 'your time is up' or you have met your nemesis or doom. The application of such a phrase is general and not restricted to Sikhs or people with turbans.

The fact is that the turban, to merrily mix images, is a red herring. The phrase that insults and annoys has nothing to do with heat or brains. It is a sexual caricature derived from the imagery of the clock-face. At twelve o'clock the hour hand and the minute hand are joined together and point vertically upwards. The implication in the shout of 'sardarji key baara bajey' is that Sikhs are unusually virile, super-sexed and sport a permanent erection. So at any hour, the penis imitates the hands of the clock in being erect. The opposite of the erect clock symbol imagery is the one of permanent droop which is used to call a male a 'chhakka', a number six.

KNOBS ON

One of the rival colleges to my own Nowrosjee Wadia College, named after the Parsi philanthropist who endowed it, was the Sir Parashurambhau or SP college, named after its founder. Then there was Fergusson College with a reputation for academic achievement much greater than that of the other two.

Our small town of Poona, known in its time as the Oxford of the East because of the number of colleges attached to the university, was for us undergraduates from all over India, dominated by the college calendar, the intercollegiate matches, the elections on campus and the entertainments at the end of the year.

One of the popular college pop bands in our years was called Russi Dinshaw and his Spare Parts. The name originated in the fact that his family owned a motor-repair garage. I don't know why the rest of the band accepted the designation, but they played reasonably merry 'covers' – imitations – of the songs on the radio's *Binaca Hit Parade*. A particular favourite, which demonstrated the skill of the gifted trumpeter, was a song called '*Tequila*', which had no lyrics except the chanted word 'Tequila' after each instrumental verse and chorus.

At the annual summer entertainment that year in the packed college hall, the audience decided out of sheer devilment to drown out the word Tequila by chanting 'Daktar Bharucha!' in unison, each time the cue for 'Tequila' came round. The good doctor, incidentally a relative by marriage into my family, had a dispensary in town and nursing home a street away from the college. Some wag started it because he thought the good doctor's name rhymed with 'Takeela!'

Another standard act, which was by popular demand repeated each year, was not one performed by members of our college. By special dispensation, the Avesti brothers, twins from SP college, were imported to play out their delightful song and dance routine. It was a Victorian music-hall song, written I now discover in 1888 by Joseph J. Sullivan. The Avestis had perfected the costume and the act to a T. They dressed in tailcoats with dress shirts and bow ties, with spats and shoes that tapped the stage. They wore the hats that the song featured, and carried hooked canes, which they used in their swinging choreography.

The first verse and chorus were:

Now how I came to get this hat, 'tis very strange and funny
Grandfather died and left to me his property and money
And when the will it was read out, they told me straight and flat
If I would have his money, I must always wear his hat'

CHORUS

'Where did you get that hat? Where did you get that tile?
Isn't it a nobby one, and just the proper style?
I should like to have one just the same as that!'
Where'er I go, they shout 'Hello! Where did you get that hat'

The word that stood out was 'nobby'. It is still very much in usage and means someone from the upper crust of society. David Cameron and his Cabinet, a surprising proportion of whom are from Eton, the elite 'public' school of England, and either from Oxford or Cambridge, are often lampooned as 'nobs'. The word has, of course, been confounded with its homophone 'knobs'.

The word nobby in the song, used as an adjective, characterizes the hat as classy, stylish, of distinction, even aristocratic.

The word is a British annexation of the Hindustani words 'nawab' and 'nawabi', meaning a ruler or king. The early British potentates of the East India Company who set themselves up in style in their Indian abodes with servants and retinue, and returned home to Britain with well-but-mostly-ill-gotten gains, were dubbed 'nabobs', not royalty but squirearchy. Hence 'nobby'.

PURITY

Blake contrasts innocence with experience when he writes the songs of each. The idea of experience wasn't, as it is in the curriculum vitae we write for ourselves, a detail of the years we have been in a trade or the expertise we have acquired in a particular field. It was the biblical idea of The Fall.

God created Adam and Eve and then, as Milton tells us with eternal and unparalleled eloquence, Satan plotted to corrupt God's innocent creation with the fruit of experience. He tempted Eve to tempt Adam into sharing an apple from the forbidden tree.

If I were revealing a holy book, it would never occur to me to present an apple, or indeed a melon as a metaphor for sex. Perhaps a banana would lend more suggestion to the metaphor, or maybe a fig. An Alphonso mango wouldn't be an adequate representation of the sexual act but could, in certain moods and catering to certain appetites, be a fulfilling substitute for it.

So experience was the knowledge of the act of procreation or, perhaps, the knowledge that sex is a very compulsive activity.

My maternal grandmother spoke no English, apart from a few transactional words such as 'yes' and 'no' and 'that's enough!'. Curiously though, two words associated with innocence and experience had become part of her standard vocabulary.

She would spend her evenings with other ladies of her generation sitting on the verandas or in the tiny front gardens of each other's houses on chairs, discussing this or that.

I don't think this august company concerned itself with the politics of foreign nations, but they certainly read the *Jam-e-Jamshed*, the Parsi newspaper in Gujarati, and possibly discussed the movements of royalty and the appointments to this or that office of the ladies and gentlemen of the Parsi community. Then there were, I am sure, topics such as the prohibition of alcohol, which must have come up for debate or disagreement.

Hovering around these councils as a child – my grandmother died when I was eight years old – I vaguely appreciated the fact that the main topics of conversation were recipes for sweets and pickles, the price of vegetables and eggs, the gossip of the neighbourhood, which included news of visiting relatives from Bombay or elsewhere, and the fortunes and misfortunes of other neighbours and members of the community. These included pregnancy, birth, marriage proposals, marriages, illnesses, bankruptcies and deaths.

Marriage prospects and the contracting and match-making were of particular interest, and one of the phrases in English that my grandmother and her companions used was 'innocent and ignorant'. This was applied to young, possibly marriageable girls and was a high compliment. It meant that

the particular girl was virtuous and ignorant of all that went
on in the Garden of Eden and, of course, to a large extent,
in our far-from-saintly neighbourhood.

LOVABLE ROGUES

In *A Winter's Tale*, Shakespeare creates the unforgettable Autolycus. Unlike the jesters of pre-Shakespearean drama, who amused the audience with jests as a sort of sideshow to or during the plays, Shakespeare integrates his clowns and jesters into the plot of the play, giving them the role of significant commentary or ironic undercutting of the characters in the comedies and even tragedies being played out on stage.

King Lear's Fool is the representative of captive, suffering wisdom. Autolycus, not exactly a clown, is a lovable rogue. He is a pedlar, has gone through several circumstances in his vagabond life and is now a cheat and pickpocket. He is the displaced rural peasant of Shakespeare's time, trying to hustle his way in the world.

Three to four hundred years after Shakespeare created Autolycus, several characters reminiscent of this creation, in the altogether different location of India, were brought alive. The bumpkin who comes to the city and is bewildred by its bustle and commerce is the staple hero of very many Indian films of the 1940s, '50s and after.

Raj Kapoor, the genius of popular Indian cinema, created

variations on this theme in several of his films, notably *Awaara* and the idiomatically named *Shree 420*.

The heroes of both films are wanderers and vagabonds, the first one an innocent abroad and the other one who has learnt the tricks of urban survival but is uncorrupted by them.

Raj Kapoor was, on screen, the innocent clown, the small man in oversized clothes in a big world and was, as he acknowledges, inspired by the creations of Charlie Chaplin.

Whether Kapoor was acquainted with Shakespeare's Autolycus one can't say. Nevertheless, Raj the wanderer comes to Mumbai wearing a Western coat and hat, as an updated Chaplin may have, carrying a Dick Whittington bundle on a stick. He goes through his comic adventures and sides with the poor of the city against their exploiters and, of course, wins – this isn't *King Lear*, but very significantly it is the beginning of Bollywood and its myths.

The name Raj Kapoor gives his hero is Shree 420. The number became idiomatic in India for swindlers, deceivers and tricksters. It derives from Section 420 of the Indian Penal Code, formulated in 1860, the year that Prime Minister Disraeli offered the Jewel in the Crown to Queen Victoria, making her Empress of India. The Section specifically mentions that the alleged felon be tried for the unlawful acquisition of property. The law applied to petty thieves and pickpockets. The phrase 420 has passed into Hindustani as has the phrase 'wide-boy' in English for rogues. Yet there is in the phrase, undoubtedly assisted by Raj Kapoor's adoption of it for his hero Raj, some tolerant excuse if not affection for what the Indian newspapers would call a 'miscreant'.

ROWDY SHEETERS

The euphemism for 'black money', itself a metaphorical name for money that criminally avoids paying tax, is *'do number'*, or second-grade cash. A criminal who has been charged by the police and has his details recorded on charge-sheet ten is known as a *'duss numbri'*, a ten-number man. I have only recently heard of criminals convicted of affray or domestic violence referred to as 'rowdy-sheeters' – derived, of course, from being charge-sheeted for 'rowdiness', which seems to take the edge off the nastiness of their crimes.

ROADSIDE ROMEOS

The Indian Penal Code probably doesn't enshrine the phrase, but the newspapers always referred to men who were arrested and prosecuted for verbally molesting or propositioning women on the streets as 'roadside Romeos'. The crime of passing provocative, suggestive or importuning remarks became known by the phrase, so the report might say 'he was arrested for Roadside Romeo'.

The phrase was modified for some reason and the misdemeanour became known as 'Eve-teasing'. Neither of these phrases carried the connotations of their literary or biblical originals. Romeo's love was surely consensual as Juliet desired him as passionately as he wanted her. And calling a molester an Eve-teaser inverts the equation of guilt as in the Bible it is Eve who does the tempting.

I admit that though none of them were arrested for the offence, some of the friends I associated with as a teenager would shout remarks complimenting or teasing girls who passed us on the street. It wasn't terribly offensive and was even intended as admiration at a distance. 'Wow what a walk!'

in Hindustani, or if the girl were carrying a red parasol and
walked a few yards away the parasol would be addressed and
instructed to retrace its steps and return: '*Ai chhatri, vaapis!*'

SMALL BALL

In the screenplay I wrote for the film *Bandit Queen*, an old eminent bandit fears that the heroine's actions will bring the wrath not of the less competent police, but of the army down on them. He calls the army the 'milty', an obvious and demotic corruption of 'military'.

In English, the word is used nowadays more as an adjective than as a noun – as in 'military objective' or 'military strategy'. Though not incorrect, one wouldn't say we sent the military into the Falklands, though one would say the 'military presence in Helmand'.

In the Hindustani, 'milty' is the noun and also an adjective when used to describe an army settlement or territory. A smaller section of the milty was no doubt what my character, the old bandit, had in mind. He would have referred to a detachment of twenty or so men with firepower stalking through the jungle in search of bandits as a 'paltan'. The word is a distortion of platoon, the smaller unit of a couple of dozen infantrymen under the command of a junior officer. Four or five of these platoons form a company, which then joins with two others to make a regiment. The word originates from the French word for a small ball called a 'pelote'. That this word became a metaphor for a small gathering of people and then for a detachment of soldiers is something languages mysteriously do.

In English, the word has retained its military connotation and is not used for gatherings of other sorts. In Indian usage, it can describe a gathering of other sorts. I have heard a collection of patients in a hospital yard, crossing it on crutches, described by a hospital orderly as a 'marizon ki paltan' – a mobile collection of invalids.

So also, I have heard a row of prisoners or petty criminals arrested for ticketless travel or some minor misdemeanour, being tied together by ropes and walked in a line on a railway platform referred to by the ticket collector as a 'kaydiyon ki paltan', a platoon of prisoners. There is, of course, the word commonly used in the Indian army by the non-commissioned officers to describe the recruits they are training before they are dignified with the appellation of 'jawan'. They are, in this diminished status of recruits, derisively called 'rangroots'.

Another military term, a rank which has been fascinatingly transformed into a first name for a Sikh boy, is 'General'. Punjabi friends tell me that it is rendered as 'Jarnail', a name which is common enough and one I mistook for some derivation from Sanskrit. Trust the Sikh parents, who probably have deep military traditions, to avoid any versions of lieutenant, major, colonel or brigadier and go straight for the top. I don't suppose that the rank of Field Marshal can yield a plausibly Punjabi-sounding name.

COOLIES

After completing my undergraduate studies in Cambridge, I came to London. I was in my early twenties. My father had a contract job in Iran and consequently there wasn't a family home in India to return to. Besides, my degree which was half in quantum physics didn't offer very many prospects of employment. The other half, which was in English, got me a job as a schoolteacher.

I hadn't been in a British school before but even so the Inner London Education Authority whom I approached for a job readily took me on and shipped me to a school called Henry Thornton in South London.

One of the classes I was timetabled to teach was called 3X and of the thirty pupils in it, twenty-six were black and of Caribbean descent. One wiry little lad, call him Ariel, seemed to rule the rest of the class. He was small but in the days to come, as I tried to settle this unruly mob into learning what I had to teach, it became clear that his authority over even the larger lads emanated from the fact that his family was known in South London as tough criminals and gunmen.

The class seemed resistant to the idea that an Indian was

to teach them English. It may have seemed something of an anomaly to them. I can't pretend that I had an easy time at first with 3X. They were rebellious and contemptuous of my authority, and a few days into my being with them, the class, under the tutelage of Ariel started chanting 'Coolie bhasha' at me.

At first I didn't understand the phrase and challenged one or two of them. I didn't understand it as being denigratory or racist. I just thought the chant, even if it arose twice in the hour, was a nuisance and an unwarranted interruption to the reading and study of *Lord of the Flies*.

It seemed to offend Ariel that I wasn't rising to the bait. My equanimity puzzled him and he attempted to challenge me by shouting the phrase two or three times when I turned my back to write on the blackboard.

'What are you trying to say, Ariel?' I demanded.

'You teaching us English and you are coolie bhasha,' he said. I got it.

The class was tense and silent, anticipating a dramatic confrontation.

'Who taught you those words?'

Ariel was standing now and looking for the approval of the rest of the class.

'My grandmother,' he said.

'Do you know what it means?' I asked.

'Yes! That you don't know English,' he said.

'Not quite. "Coolie" is a racial word that black Caribbeans use for Caribbean people who in Trinidad, Guyana and, of course, Jamaica, come from India. It's a rude word. Like me or worse, a white person, calling you the "N" word, which is what the racists used to call black people like you. In India, it is used for a labourer, someone who earns his money by handling baggage at railway stations, for instance. There is no shame in working hard with the sweat of your brow. Coolie is not really a dirty word unless it comes out of a dirty mouth. And the word "bhasha" is the Hindi, the Indian word for language. So what your grandmother was probably saying was that I am a coolie and speak an Indian language and you ought to shout that at me to remind me not to try and teach you English.'

Ariel wasn't expecting any of this. He shifted his weight from foot to foot and then, without a word, walked out of the class. The rest of them were silent.

'Shall we get on with the lesson now?'

We did. Ariel, for several reasons, abandoned his antagonistic stance and, eventually, we became friends and allies.

TIME PAST AND TIME PRESENT...

Peanuts are also known as monkey nuts. On the Indian streets they are known as 'sayngh-daana', 'singh' or in western India as 'moong-phali'. Together with 'chana', unhusked round lentils, peanuts, shelled and unshelled, are traditionally sold on the street on handcarts or on the side of the street on mats. In my childhood, the street-vendor carried a stand made of straw wound into a sort of double-conical figure of eight on top of which he placed the tray of nuts he transported on his head.

The more enterprising or affluent of the traders who sold the ready-shelled nuts would have an earthen pot the size of two widely cupped palms filled with burning coal to place on top of the conical heap of nuts. The ones just under the pot would be hot and dispensable to customers in 'waste' paper, each sheet loosely recycled by hand into a conical receptacle. Lots of cones.

The other forms in which peanuts were sold were unshelled ones, which had been roasted or boiled in salt water till their shells were soft.

Then, at the age of sixteen, I went to Bombay to enlist in the university department of chemical technology. The zeitgeist of the times induced my generation to try to acquire academic qualifications that led to 'fields with scope'. This meant in general professions and industries that were being established at the time in India. Engineering and branches of medicine were much favoured and since my family had a tradition of being builders and engineers, I was induced to apply for a university place in an elite department with students from all over India.

In Bombay I lived with my granduncle an hour or more's journey by train and longer by tram to Matunga, where the department was located. The local trains were normally crowded but my journeys were contra to the flow into the city in the mornings and out of it in the evenings. Even so, the commuter trains were packed and at most stops beggars, singers, vendors of horse-racing fixture cards, toys and baubles and peanuts would get in, shout for alms or advertise their wares and pass through from compartment to compartment.

The peanut vendors, with the nuts wrapped neatly in the recycled paper cones carried in cloth bags on their shoulders, had invented a peculiar name for the monkey nuts. Instead of shouting 'peanuts' or 'moong-phali' they would pass through the compartments shouting 'time pass!' – a name the commuters adopted. It was an apt description. For some whose journeys from one end of the line to the other may take two hours, the shelling and consumption of a cone of monkey nuts would help pass the empty time.

I may have resorted to passing my travelling time to and from college in this way, but my main resource to stave off the boredom of the course and profession, for which it soon became clear to me I could muster no enthusiasm, was reading.

I read any and every paperback I could afford from the new and second-hand pavement booksellers. I read everything from the speeches of Lenin to the cases and detective work of Perry Mason, Earl Stanley Gardner's sleuth-barrister. The work that had the most impact on me was Lawrence Durrell's Alexandria Quartet. I read all four books on the trains and trams to and from my lectures on chemical engineering, and by the time I'd read the fourth book, I felt ready to abandon those studies and contemplate taking up writing for a living. It was a strong but impossible ambition and one that I dared not, for years, admit except to close friends with similarly dreamy aims and no prospects. The passing of that year is, in my mind, associated with the reading I did and with the flavour and function of the peanuts on commuter trains.

SICK MAN'S FOOD

The first Mughal Emperor – or marauder, depending upon your historical bias – Zair-ud-din Babur remarked in his memoir, the *Baburnama*, that the land he had conquered, Hindustan, had very few gardens or the sorts of luscious fruit he was used to from the Central Asian lands of the Oxus. His other complaint was that Indians were peculiar in their culinary habits because they ate 'grain with grain'. He meant that Indians eat daal with rice or daal with chappatis, whereas a sturdy fellow who had assumed the title of Babur, meaning tiger, needed meats with his rice or wheat. He must have considered the diet of rice and daal the diet of the debilitated.

My grandmother, following long established tradition, certainly did. Parsis are no vegetarians, but when one fell ill the prescribed meal for a few days towards recovery was 'khichdi' – a simple mixture of boiled daal and rice flavoured with turmeric, which was supposed to have medicinal qualities, with onions and maybe one or other spice such as cinnamon. It was sick man's food, served in our house with the daal remaining grainy rather than becoming a gravy. That's not to say that khichdi was exclusively a convalescent food. It was also on the normal menu, served up with relish as part of the household's regular diet, always accompanied by dried Bombay duck patio, a sweet and sour 'curry' or with a 'saahs', a sort of whitish well-spiced gravy with chunks of fish and tomatoes.

Why the British adopted it as a breakfast food is not too clear, but they called it 'kedgeree' and though their recipe contained lentils and rice, it also contained fish or meat or chopped-up boiled eggs. This precluded it being accompanied by any sauce. It was a meal in itself and not thought of as a sick person's diet. It became the British equivalent of a Spanish paella or even an elaborate Italian risotto.

The word kedgeree retains a literal usage in English whereas in Hindustani or Gujarati it has acquired the metaphoric meaning for an unwieldy amalgam, a mixture or a muddle.

In the worst case, it could mean a mess.

The key to this usage is probably not the contempt that someone like Babur would have placed on the grain-with-grain nature of it, but rather on the combined nature, which made a discrete definition between one thing and another difficult if not impossible. That was the entropic nature of khichdi!

BACK TO BASICS

You see it most in Indian official letters and e-mails and hear it most often in official or bureaucratic phone calls and conversations with Indian secretaries and administrators – the word 'revert'. It may be a request as in 'please revert' or a promise or statement of intent as in, 'I will revert.'

It means send me an answer or I will send you a decision or reply.

The English dictionary meaning and, indeed, the none-too-frequent English usage of 'revert' is to return to the place from whence you came, literally or metaphorically. One may revert to one's former self, for instance. It has never meant 'send me a reply', or been part of an intention to answer a query.

It may well be that the often used English phrase 'get back' used in the sense of 'please get back to me' or 'I shall get back to you with plans or a reply', etc., has been mistaken for getting back to a former state. Hence the literal 'revert', which does mean 'get back' in one sense, has been substituted in Indian communications for the idiomatic English 'get back'.

If you disagree, kindly revert.

CLOTHING

The French word for a loose shirt is 'chemise', which is undoubtedly the Europeanization of 'khamiz', Hindustani for the same garment. The name 'Jodh-purrs' for horse-riding trousers tight around the calves and ankles, probably has its origin in the uniform worn by polo players in Rajasthan.

My grandfather would sing a song in his bath, which was probably the first expression of melancholy I had experienced at the age of two or three. It went:

'Tu purdah-nasheen ka ashiq hein
Yuun naam-e-waffa barbaad na kar…'

The 'purdah-nasheen' addressed in the song is the veiled beloved and the 'purdah', the veil, is the barrier of modesty, which the lover seeks to overcome.

In English the word is used, for instance, to suspend an operation or a process as in, 'The plans have been put in purdah till next year'. The word has come to mean a limbo.

I suppose the lover who is prevented from seeing the face of his beloved can be said to be in a romantic limbo.

THE DOG IT WAS

My uncle was an engineer and a building contractor in Mumbai, and as part of the conventions of his business, had to keep on the right side and in the favour of architects who handed out building contracts. No doubt most of them in the trade would take a cut from the builder they chose to execute their projects, prestigious or otherwise. He worked with a particular architect and used to mix with him socially, in the course of which he found out that the architect's wife and young daughters loved dogs and were anxious to take in a new one.

My uncle duly went to the best dog show and bought the prize-winning one, which that year happened to be a fox-terrier. The animal came with a distinguished certificate of pedigree and with the unwieldy name which its breeders, in the style of the naming of racehorses, had given it. The puppy was grandiloquently called Diwali Cracker of Vaigunga. Not the sort of name you can call a puppy when training it.

My uncle presented the puppy, with his long muzzle and brown and white patched coat, to the architect's daughters who were toddlers and infants themselves. They duly named him Bruno and were very happy with their new pet. Not for long. Bruno bit everyone in the house when he felt he had been provoked. And even when he hadn't. He bit the mistress of the house, the master, the servants and the children. The architect was least pleased and asked my uncle to take the dog back or face the option of him being put down. My uncle took Bruno in.

At the time, he lived in a small Mumbai flat and he and his young wife spent their days working. The accommodation and their routines were not conducive to keeping pets and my uncle duly brought Bruno down to Pune to his father's house, where I lived with my grandfather and his two daughters, my aunts. Our house already had three dogs and a fourth could be fed and kept with very little rice and few bones added to the daily dog menu. My uncle was firmly of the opinion that the architect's family had mistreated the dog and that Bruno was really mild and misunderstood and would behave himself perfectly.

This was true up to a point. In many ways he behaved himself but he did bite selected people in his first few days and weeks with us. He bit my cousin, he bit my friends, he bit my aunts and my sister. The only two people he never assaulted were myself and Hukam Ali who fed him, brushed him, bathed him and played with him, teaching him to fetch sticks and punctured tennis balls. Both Hukam Ali and I undertook to train Bruno to obey the command to sit, to follow, to desist from growling and, of course, to answer to his name.

This last bit of instruction had an element of schizophrenia. The household called him Bruno, but Hukam Ali, through some quirk of culture or construction of mouth, couldn't pronounce 'Bruno'. He would, no matter how diligently we tried to explain how the double consonant sounded or was formed, pronounce Bruno as 'bulloona'. My friends and I would ask him to say 'brick' and he would render it as 'bilick'. If we conceded that he found 'r' difficult or impossible to get his tongue around after 'b', we would ask him to pronounce 'black', which he delivered – quite willingly and even amused to take the tests – as 'bilak'. The name Bulloona soon wedged the name Bruno out. Everyone began to refer to the dog as Bulloona, or Blooney. So 'come on, Bruno' became a clarion call, only it was pronounced 'khiman Blooney!'

———

My ayah Chandrabai had a particular, mysterious way of interpreting English pronunciation. I have asked speech trainers and diction therapists for an explanation, but they remain as puzzled as I have always been. My first example of her deviation is understandable as it's a distortion that makes some sense. When my sister and I were infants and Chandrabai was partially in charge, my mother would sing a nursery rhyme which went:

'Bye, baby Bunting,
Daddy's gone a-hunting,
Gone to get a rabbit skin
To wrap the baby Bunting in'

Chandrabai's version to the same tune began in Hindi: 'Soja Baby Soja', but it distorted into a linguistic mixture and the last line emerged as 'Ratna baby Bunchhee!' Neither my sister nor I are called Ratna, though it is a girl's name.

The distortion which has no feasible explanation is her transformation of the word 'bulb'. In trying to pronounce it she would say 'kooloop'. How the 'b' became a 'k' no Professor Henry Higgins can explain.

LORD AND MASTER

The term 'mea domina', meaning a lady who dominates as a lordly mistress, was born in chivalric times when language conceded this concession to women as a means of demonstrating the faux-humility of the male gender. The word 'madam', born from the phrase, has, of course picked up various connotations in various contexts. The madam or Madame of a bawdy house is literally a pimp. Not dignified perhaps, but certainly with masterly position over her girls.

The East India Company sent out Englishmen to India in the seventeenth century and they were universally distinguished as 'sahibs'. The Urdu word meaning 'lord and master' comes from the Arabic 'sahiba', which is the much more friendly term meaning friend or companion. The sahibs weren't accompanied at first by womenfolk. Until the early eighteenth century, bringing wives and families to India was not considered safe or desirable but as the traders began to settle, the European womenfolk accompanied them. These ladies were addressed as 'madam sahibs', which was then shortened to ma'am and later, 'memsahibs'.

The usage was restricted in the main to European ladies.

Indian ladies, however grand, retained their appellations of Begum Sahiba or Shrimatiji.

The term memsahib was used in addressing European ladies by all ranks and, notably, by the retinues of domestic servants, and the term at the time certainly contained a tone of subservience. In recent times, though, there has been a shrinkage of the usage. One notices that Indian shopkeepers, tradesmen and even domestic help have stopped using the word and gone back to the less subservient, but just as polite and respectful, 'Madam'. It's universally used for all races, not just for the Europeans who originally merited the title.

NOISES OFF

Sometimes doggies say bow-wow and sometimes they say woof-woof. Cats always say meow and sheep bleat, but that's the name of the sound which is more meh-eh-eh. That's, of course, in English.

The verb in Hindustani for a dog barking, which supposedly imitates the sound of the bark, is 'bhonkna'.

The sound of laughter in English, from the universal 'ha ha' to the slyer 'heh heh' and the expression of sly or mocking glee in 'hee hee' to the pompous announcement of Santa Claus who says 'ho ho ho', is rendered in several registers almost always beginning with exhalation of the 'h'. This last has, however, run into trouble as the syllable 'ho' has been transformed in Afro-American street usage to mean a whore. In certain places, the actors playing Santas were told to modify the sound of their laugh in case the woman present felt insulted.

One of the dialects that the art of the comic book invented or evolved was the attribution of sounds to actions or phenomena.

The sound of a punch or a hard knock with the fist was

always rendered as 'SOCK', 'WHAM' or 'POW', written in capital letters with exclamation marks and stars for emphasis. In reality, the sound of bare knuckle on flesh would be more like a soft 'thkk'. But then myth cannot be burdened by realism. If the blow wasn't with a naked fist and entailed the use of a plank or a more hurtful non-explosive weapon, the sound would be rendered as 'SMACK' or even 'WALLOP'. Both these words rendering sounds are nouns and verbs. 'I smacked him' or 'walloped him' or even 'gave him a tight smack', are acceptable, if not stylish, usage.

The sound of a gun in the comic book lexicon was 'bang bang' and that of a machine gun was variously 'rat-a-tat-tat' and 'budda-budda-budda' in big sharp-cornered letters scrawled across the frame of the comic in garish colours or in black. The actual sound of gunfire is better represented by the syllable 'dhop' or 'dhomp', if it's a heavier gun or, 'tthor' if it's at a distance. But the convention of the comic takes us back to 'bang bang' and the single word is now the noun for an explosion. I heard a loud 'bang', or even 'the beginning of the universe, characterized by cosmologists as the Big Bang'.

The gangster movie, and curry-Western, came late to Bollywood. The films of the first sixty or so years of Indian cinema may have portrayed squabbles, scuffles and even bloody physical disputes, but the imitation of the blood and violence of Western movies only set in later. Scenes of gunfire, of the wiping out of rivalry through Al Capone-style operations in cars and encounters in warehouses, only came about when the entertainment value of the new myths of urban violence were born. The phrase used to characterize these films was supposedly the audio-incarnation of fisticuffs: 'DHISHOOM DHISHOOM'.

And now, ironically, there are restaurants in Britain called Dishoom, with perhaps an intentional suggestion of dishes. I suppose it's not that absurd – after all, the British call sausages 'bangers' and there could very well be a sausage-serving restaurant called Bang.

NO CONVULSION

The male West Indian youth of Britain describe a female whom they think is well-proportioned or physically sexy as, 'fit'.

The term doesn't describe any quality of personality, character, intelligence or beauty of any sort apart from face and figure – and is probably more orientated towards an appreciation of the latter.

In India, the English word seems to be a term of acceptance, agreement or approval. In several situations, having outlined a plan or a strategy, the response is 'fit!' It has come to mean more than 'okay'. It means, 'this covers every eventuality'.

A common Indian phrase a film-director friend of mine has adopted is 'no issues!'

The term 'fit' comes from being certified as healthy. The term 'no issues' from the practice in the Bollywood industry of the constant presence of financial and production problems which do raise troublesome issues. 'No issues' is the term which invites you to move to the next consideration, which in terms of script, production or finance, may produce some.

YES GOODBYE

The highways of India, still in large measure roads which are hardly more than a single lane with dusty sides so that vehicles have to drive half off the tarmacked road when passing an oncoming vehicle, are crowded with trucks.

The trucks are responsible for a very large proportion of freight in the subcontinent and now, through the agency of the overworked and often reckless truck drivers, for most road deaths and even for the spread of AIDS.

In *Hind Swaraj*, Mahatma Gandhi's early work, he blamed the establishment of the railways by the British in India as a means of spreading theft and venereal disease. The Mahatma may have overstated the case or, indeed, pushed an idiosyncratic point of view, but the statistic connecting the spread of AIDS to the national mileage of trucks and their drivers is not a perverse fantasy. Away from home for weeks or longer, and with the monotony and hardship of a life on the road, they avail of the services of sex workers. The network of their contacts expands geometrically and the spread of HIV can be, and has been traced, though by no means exclusively, largely to them as carriers.

Truck drivers are also, not surprisingly, accused of causing most accidents through drug abuse. Though they speak no English, I have heard them using Western slang for ganja, cocaine and heroin, alluding to them as 'blow', 'Charlie' and 'smack'.

Truck drivers have no friends among the rest of India's road users. They are, for the most part, badly behaved and use the bulk of their trucks to bully other traffic, driving down the centres of roads, occupying two lanes of highways, overtaking from the wrong side, shining their headlights into oncoming traffic with no care for their blinding effect, riding lighter traffic off the roads and a hundred other manifestations of bad road manners and practice.

These bad habits and the lack of order and etiquette are not about to change and there is no agency that treats the problem as urgent. Older than the convention of bad or selfish driving is the legend, subject to variations, on the back of all trucks. Most of them in any order or combination sport the words 'HORN', 'OK', 'TATA' and 'PLEASE'. These words, painted prominently on the back of trucks to be legible to drivers behind them predate any manufacture of trucks by the Tata Engineering and Locomotive Company (TELCO).

The legend is embossed onto trucks that have not been manufactured by the Tata conglomerates or affiliates.

The slogan of the road has nothing to do with the manufacturer or brand name of the truck. It arose from the early use of the roads by lorries. There was, in those days, an order to the words, which has been subsequently lost, as has the meaning of the slogan. Today, a lorry painter will oblige by blessing the truck with the words in any random order as a sort of talisman of the road.

Originally, the words were arranged as 'HORN PLEASE. OK? TATA.'

The purpose of the writing was to request the vehicle behind the truck carrying it to blow their horn with a request to overtake. The driver of the truck would then stick his arm out of the cab and signal the vehicle behind with a series of waves when it was okay to pass. It was assumed that the vehicle behind would act on the hand signal, overtake and go its faster way. The slogan on the truck politely said farewell with the final 'Ta ta', meaning 'bye-bye'.

INCLUSION OR INTRUSION?

Our generation was rightly taught Hindi as a compulsory subject in schools. It was the era of the late 1950s and the educational policy that universally imposed Hindi on the school curriculum met with resistance in south India. The attempt to make this formalized, purged-of-Urdu and Sanskritized version of the demotic Hindustani the central official language threw up its anomalies.

In school, we ridiculed the attempt to manufacture words for ordinary usage. Our uniform required us to wear school ties each day. The contrived Hindi word for tie, which has never been used by anyone but passed into the lexicon of schoolboy humour, was 'kanth langot'. The double entendre, with the word sounded like the English 'c word', appealed to us as we could say the forbidden homophonic first word of the phrase now with impunity, and would exchange words about adjusting each other's 'kanth langots', inserting the phrase into English sentences.

Other words and phrases, which were said to have been invented but never used, were held up as objects of fun – phrases such as kana phoos-phoos for a telephone and 'agni ratha soochaka tambra loha patika' for a railway signal. Even then we must have realized that these were probably the work of satirists rather than the genuine efforts of the committees entrusted with fabricating a new vocabulary. Ties are still 'ties', as are the words for telephones and signals. English words have passed without question smoothly into Hindustani.

If these adopted words are nouns which signify inventions such as 'computer', 'mobile phone', 'TV set', 'programme' or 'company', it seems natural that there are no fabricated or pretentious purist substitutes seeking to displace them. With abstractions such as culture, corruption, customs, tradition, one hears and learns the proper Hindi usage usually from television. Speaking on TV, a presenter may use the term 'bhrashtachar' for corruption, but a participant in a Hindi debate may equally use the word 'corruption' and be understood by the co-participants and the home audience.

There are some English abstract nouns which have fascinatingly been integrated into regular speech. One of these is the word 'tension'. Used in its psychological sense, as mental stress or worry, it has passed into the dialect of the tribe. You can hear 'tension mat ley yaar', meaning 'don't get stressed', or even 'theek hain koi tension nahin' meaning, 'that's fine, no issues involved'.

The word, picked up by Bollywood, is incorporated in the dialogue line 'tension leyne ka nahin, tension deyne ka', which means, 'don't accept tension, dish it out!'

In north India, where Urdu was born, the language retains its distinction and dignity. In western India, where I grew up, Hindi, Urdu and the colloquial amalgam, best known as Hindustani, prevails and is distorted into a form known as 'Bumbaia Hindi'. This is a mixture with English and Marathi words thrown in.

My Urdu vocabulary grew to a humble extent when, late in life, I became a fan of ghazals and qawwalis, had friends who interpreted them for me, bought dictionaries to help decipher the meanings and listened incessantly to the likes of Ustad Nusrat Fateh Ali, the Sabri brothers and a hundred others.

The lyrics were interpreted for me as being 'pure' – the works of Amir Khusrau being pre-Urdu compositions with verses in demotic Prakrit and the choruses in Persian. No English intruded.

One very popular qawwali, sung by various artists, was the tribute to Shahbaaz Qalandar, the Sufi mystic of Sewan in Sind. Its chorus goes *'Damadam mast Qalandar, Ali Shahbaaz Qalandar'*. Then the surprising intrusion, *'Ali da pehla number!'* The word 'number', completely and seamlessly integrated into the fabric of the song's meaning, metre and rhyme scheme, is still a foreign intrusion. So when was the lyric composed and was it subsequently modified after English words began to be incorporated even into Sufi tributes to a thirteenth-century saint?

———

That English words intruded into popular Hindi film songs is not surprising. They were mostly added for farcical effect.

One song from my childhood, sung by a comic character making up to a woman he loves, went:

> *Meri jaan, meri jaan*
> *Sunday key Sunday aana*
> *Meri jaan, meri jaan,*
> *Sunday key Monday.*
>
> *I love you!*
>
> (Oh my love, oh my love
> Please meet me on a Sunday
> My darling, my darling
> A Sunday or a Monday…
> I love you)

Then the woman addressed continues the song with the dismissive line: '*Bhaag yahan sey door!*' Which means 'Get away from me!'

The song progressed with the suitor promising her whisky and brandy and then absurdly saying he will feed her hens' eggs if she will only be his! I don't suppose the eggs were considered a tempting delicacy, as perhaps champagne and caviar might have been, but they were intruded into the lyric because the Hindi word for egg, 'unday', rhymes with Sunday and Monday.

———

Another nonsensical rhyme, which my cousins' ayah had

picked up or invented, used the shortened name of Jamsetji
Jeejeebhoy, a Parsi whose family made a fortune from the
Sino-British opium trade and who was consequently given
the title of baronet by the Raj. The song went:

Jamsoo Jeejeebhoy
Jamsoo Jeejeebhoy
Thaajo chhumno sooko boomlo
Kawaab ney kutleys!'

(Jamshed Jeejeebhoy
A fresh pomfret, a dried Bombay Duck
A kebab and a hamburger)

It continues nonsensically:

Jamsoo Jeejeebhoy
Jamsoo Jeejeebhoy
Suwthhy pehllo suwthhy chhello
My dear biskeet!

(Jamshed Jeejeebhoy
The first of all, the last of all
My dear, biscuit!)

Of course, it makes less sense than cows jumping over
moons or dishes running away with spoons, but it served its
purpose of regaling children with the nonsense they have to
learn to recognize as such to live in the real world.

TOWERS

Despite being merely eight years old when my grandmother died, I insisted on following on foot – as the males of our Parsi community do – the funeral procession which carries the corpse to the towers of silence. These were perhaps six miles away and the procession, all men in white, passed through the town and across Golibar Maidan, the gunshot field, to the stone wells standing twenty or so feet high where the dead are deposited.

The ritual of placing dead bodies on a mesh in these towers to be consumed by vultures, with the bones falling into the centre, a communal grave, was initiated in a Zoroastrian period after the days of the Achaemenid Empire. The emperors of this dynasty, Cyrus, Darius and Xerxes, all have marked tombs – two of them with decorations depicting their historical deeds. There is evidence, from Herodotus and from archaeological finds, that ossuaries or pits for the depositing of bones existed in the fourth and fifth centuries BC. For royalty and the aristocracy, the practice of disposing of the dead by leaving bodies open to scavenging animals may have coexisted with the practice of burial.

The general practice of this form of disposal must have arisen in the bleak days after Alexander the Damned, the Macedonian warlord, defeated Darius III in 326 BC and left the Persian Empire devastated and prey to marauders from Central Asia. The revival of the Zoroastrian Persian Empire under the Sassanians took place in the third century AD, and there is evidence that this ecologically economical practice of disposal of the dead was prevalent in their dynastic reign and beyond.

The Parsi Zoroastrians, who fled Persia after the Islamic conquest of the seventh century had replaced the Sassanian dynasty, brought the ritual to India. They constructed the towers for the disposal of the dead and called them 'dokhmas'.

In 1832, after the British had established a presence in India, Robert Murphy, a translator to the colonial government of the East India Company, coined the phrase 'towers of silence', an apt and forbidding name as the grinding sound the vultures make when carving out the flesh of the dead is not loud enough to be heard from the ground below the tower. When the name arose is not known, but it may have been around the end of the seventeenth century when the British began, with the help of Parsi builders and tradesmen, to establish ports and cities such as Bombay.

I was aware of how my community disposed of our dead even before my grandmother was placed on the forbidding towers. The knowledge was the stuff of very many nightmares. It was, however, only in very recent years that I have heard the practice referred to as 'sky-burial'. The practice is native to Tibet as well and has been called 'sky-burial' in translation of Buddhist texts. In India this practice is threatened by the near-extinction of vultures – a consequence of them feeding on the remains of animals that had been treated with Diclofenac, a drug poisonous to birds. Its use, now banned for Indian cattle, has wiped out ninety per cent of India's vulture population.

So the practice of sky-burial in India is threatened and the short-lived phrase will be relegated to history with it.

IN YOUR COURT

The British allude to the male genitalia in several ways. The pantomime phrase would be 'crown jewels'. There are various other euphemisms including the folk term 'cock and balls'. The various words for penis from dick, tool and pecker to prick and todger, are probably all derived from Anglo-Saxon and owe nothing to the subcontinent.

The word for testicles that does owe its origin to Hindustani is 'ghoulies'. In English usage one would, for instance, say 'he kicked him in the ghoulies'. The word is the anglicized distortion of the word 'golis', which in Hindustani means marbles or round things such as pills. It's pronounced in Hindustani as the shortening of goalkeeper – a goalie. The English pronunciation has picked up an 'oo' sound and the ghoul is pronounced as in a spectre. The 'oo' may have been incorporated as the poetic addition of the sound of pain that follows being kicked in them.

AIEE SHUDDUP, YAAR

I stick to the belief that the phrase 'aiee shuddup, yaar!' was invented in some north Indian university, probably Delhi.

It isn't simply a command to shut one's mouth. 'Shut up', or 'shut the fuck up!', is very clear. These phrases can be used in jest, or to tell someone to stop singing, or rendered in a menacing tone which implies grave displeasure and the absolute prohibition against the pronouncement or against venturing to mention the subject.

The Indian phrase, bracketing shut up with 'aiee' and 'yaar', has the subtler implications of 'I don't believe what you are saying' or 'that is totally incredible' and even 'how can fate treat me this way?'

Two stories to illustrate:

When I worked as a TV executive, commissioning programmes for Channel 4 UK, I had routine dealings concerning visas and permissions for filming with the Indian High Commission. I was very friendly with the minister for information, as their press attaché was called. The post was occupied by successive foreign service personnel, all of whom were appointed to the position as a step on their way to ambassadorships or higher postings. One gentleman with whom I became friendly was very distinctly north Indian, a Delhi-ite, and always spoke in a cultivated English accent and idiom. It was a bit archaic, as though he had read a lot of P.G. Wodehouse.

Rajiv Gandhi was prime minister of India at the time and the chairman of the Commonwealth Heads of State one year. There was a raging controversy about sanctions against the South African 'apartheid regime', and Margaret Thatcher was advocating lifting sanctions to the other Commonwealth states most of whom, led by Rajiv, were in favour of maintaining and strengthening economic and political sanctions.

A pair of investigative journalists came to me with very broad, convincing and serious evidence to prove that India was breaching, clandestinely, the very sanctions she was in favour of on three or four fronts, with the connivance of government departments. India was importing diamonds from South Africa on a huge scale. It was exporting food, raw materials of particular sorts and some typically Indian manufactured goods through devious bills of lading. It was also engaged in laundering South African money, and Indian businessmen were possibly breaching the arms embargo by brokering arms sales.

It was an explosive scoop. I commissioned them to make the programme and we found ways to do it without official permission, which would, of course, not be forthcoming. The programme was ready for transmission the day before the Commonwealth Heads of State conference and Rajiv Gandhi was in London on a visit. Channel 4 Television didn't publicize the content of the investigative programme till later in the day when we would preview it on screen, but I felt impelled to alert my friend at the High Commission who would undoubtedly have to face some of the fallout after the exposure.

I got him on the phone. 'Hi, X,' I said, 'how are things?'

'Oh, swept off my feet, old chap, as the PM is here, you know and handling the protocol and the press. One has more than one's hands full.' His accent was the upper-class English he had adopted.

'Well yes, I expect so. Listen, in all fairness, I thought I should alert you to the fact that tonight we are transmitting a programme at peak time proving, conclusively, that India or Indian industries and businessmen are breaching sanctions with South Africa.'

There was a long pause. I waited for the reaction.

'Aiee shuddup yaar!' came the rejoinder in a down-to-earth Delhi University accent with no veneer of the Drone's Club. The jolly personality had given way to the underlying lad of the Delhi campus.

'I'm sorry, old bean,' I said, 'but that's what a free press is for.'

'Yes…' he said, hesitatingly. ' Umm… You didn't bother to get permissions.'

'Who would have given us permissions?'

'Right. Right,' he said and then, regaining composure and his British accent, 'Farrukh Sahib, you have to do what you have to do and I have to do what I have to do. Right now. So, see you sometime, old chap.'

We remained friends. It did not stop him becoming ambassador in his next posting.

And the second story:

A friend told me about a colleague of hers, a graduate of Delhi University who went to seek his fortune in New York. He got a night job at a petrol station in the sort of district where the workers at the tills of the station have to barricade themselves behind bars and bullet-proof plastic.

He was working a quiet night shift on his first week in the city when a grubby-looking woman, stoned out of her head, wandered up to the window through which he collected money or cards for petrol and, bleary eyed, addressed our young man.

'Gimme ten dollars and I'll give you a blow job,' she said matter-of-factly.

'Aiee shut up yaar!' was all our boy could think of saying. She staggered off into the night.

And the third:

There's a phrase I hear which is the preserve of Indian females. It means, 'I don't believe you.'

I tell my sister I am fed up of London, and that I am emigrating to Nigeria.

'I'll give you two slaps!' she says, not in the least intending any physical assault. It could even mean 'Don't be ridiculous', as in, 'Oh look, there's a tyrannosaurus easting your roses!' – 'I'll give you two slaps!'

DUST INTO DUST

The troops who had fought under Robert Clive in 1857 wore uniforms imported from Europe. The red and blue coats, the cross sashes across the breast, white canvas belts and elaborate headgear were the plumage of warriors of the day.

The life-size statue of a British soldier being devoured by a tiger, depicting Tipu Sultan's hatred of the British colonialists, in the Victoria and Albert Museum, is wearing a full infantryman's uniform.

By 1846, the local conquests by the East India Company were finished. The major wars were restricted to Afghanistan until the 'mutiny' of its own Indian sepoys broke out in 1857. The mutineers wore ceremonial uniforms too as the idea that camouflage, the utility and practical use of a uniform in warfare, hadn't pervaded the entire army. In that year, a British Indian cavalry regiment received its change of uniform from the bright reds, blues and whites of ceremony to practical colours for camouflage. The uniform chosen for them was of dull earth colour, the colour of dust, the colour that the natives called 'khaki'. Dust or dirt is 'khak' and here was the adjective to describe the colour.

The colour and functionality of the uniform didn't help win any wars in Afghanistan. Even so, with some eye to the costs of production, various regiments of the British army adopted the colour as their uniform in the Boer wars and subsequently, almost the entire British army abandoned ceremonial dress warfare and switched to khaki in the First World War.

GOODBYE, MR CHIPS

It took me some time to adjust to the fact that French fries are not the same as potato chips. They are, in fact, the result of mass-powdering potatoes, transporting the dry powder in tins, turning it into a paste, putting the paste through a sieve that turns it into strips and then deep frying. These chips are produced by cutting potatoes into the requisite crescents or elongated oblongs and then boiling them till they are half-cooked and then frying them.

Did the French paste their potatoes and turn them into 'chips'? Or is this a method invented for mass production by the fast-food industry of America?

When potatoes are thinly sliced and fried, making little crisp, warped and misshapen discs, they are called 'crisps' in Britain, but not in India. When I first arrived in Britain I didn't know what a 'crisp' was as we always knew the same crunchy potato snacks as 'wafers'. This was probably because they resembled the 'wafer' of the Catholic communion service and there was a coincidence between the introduction of Catholicism to India and the introduction of the potato.

Calling them crisps tells us about their texture; calling them wafers, about their shape.

The word chips is still used for wafers and for their finger-sized relative in India. In Britain, crisps and chips are never confused, perhaps because one names a texture and the other a shape, though a chip off any block, even a soft potato, can presumably take any shape the shaving instrument gives it.

AWAY

My fictionalized youthful autobiography is called *Poona Company*. It is a novel of a rite of passage in small-town India in the fifties and sixties, and could be read as concatenation of short stories. They are all set around my neighbourhood whose hub was a crossroads called Sarbatwalla Chowk in reality and in the book.

'Chowk' means crossroads, and it was where Sachapir Street crossed Dastur Meher Road. So much local history there. A 'sacha pir' – a truthful holy man or 'witness' – was supposed to have lived and preached under a neem tree in that vicinity in times past. The road was one that led outside what was the Poona city of the Marathas before the British got there in the eighteenth century.

Sachapir Street now connected the old city to the shopping streets of the British cantonment. The street that crossed it, near the house in which I was brought up, Dastur Meher Road was named after a Parsi high priest of the city's fire temple inaugurated in 1844. And the crossroads, formed at the junction of these, Sarbatwalla Chowk, was, according to my grandfather, the popular name given to a local liquor bar at the junction, 'sarbat' being the name for a light beverage and a euphemism for hard liquor. The word sherbet which now means a sweet in British usage, comes from the sweet cool drinks of Raj days.

My book begins with a policeman standing and directing traffic on the chowk. The nearest police station was a few furlongs away, situated at some other crossroads. It was the practice of the police force set up by the British Raj in the early twentieth century, following some of the traditions of the Mughal Empire, which had its own law enforcement agencies, to locate police stations at crossroads.

The stations were called chowkis – places on the chowk, the crossroads. They usually contained a detention cell where miscreants were kept till they were tried and let loose or sentenced. Hence the detention of drunken or miscreant British soldiers serving in Indian towns by the civil police was known as 'being in chokey'.

The official law enforcement duty of the chowk has other linguistic offshoots. All guardsmen or watchmen who act as security for offices or for a residential building are known as 'chowkidars', literally 'men of the crossroads'.

MAIDAN

In Pune, a cycle ride away from my home at the end of the main street, inevitably named Mahatma Gandhi Road, and up a small incline, was an empty square mile or more of land with an army shooting range at the end. The ground was not level and was spotted with dark, sometimes near-purple volcanic rock of the Indian peninsula's Deccan plateau. The ground, despite its unevenness was used as a playground by footballers and cricketers and served, in the darkness, as a lovers' lane for forbidden liaisons in what was then an outwardly puritanical environment.

Kissing in the street only became reluctantly acceptable when Pune was invaded by hordes of Europeans and Americans who wore orange clothes and came in their thousands to join the ashram of the charlatan who called himself Bhagwan Shree Rajneesh.

The shooting range at the end of this plot gave it its name. It was called 'Golibar-Maidan'. The word maidan is commonly used for any piece of open ground, for an empty, grassy or even desolate spot. The word comes from the Persian or Arabic *'maydan'* into Urdu and gets transformed into maidan

WORDS 149

in Hindustani. The word is a noun for the field – as in Pune's
Golibar Maidan or in Mumbai's Azad Maidan, the field of
freedom. Subsequently, the phrase 'Maidan may aajaa!' is a
challenge to enter the field of combat – a throwing down of
the gauntlet.

Whether it's a coincidence, whether one derives from
the other, or whether they emerge from the same root, the
northern European word for a piece of open ground is the
similar sounding 'midden'. In Ukrainian, a 'maidan' is literally
a square. In Danish, the word was a combination of 'mud-
dung' and came, in English, to mean a wasteland but has
accumulated a much more pleasant connotation – of a piece
of ground where people may gather.

The town west of London, called Maidenhead, is no
indication of its purity. Its 'maiden' comes not from a virgin
but from the word for a wild place, a field, a 'midden', originally
from the Scandinavian, a dump for dung and mud.

DEUS MY GOD

In one of Kipling's short stories an Englishman 'goes native'. The word around the cantonment and the club is not that he is having an affair or that he keeps one or several Indian mistresses whom he has got with child. That may have been frowned upon, but on the Christian principle of not casting the first stone, would be overlooked. No, his transgression is real sin. He has not embraced the native women, he has embraced the native gods. He has turned his back on the true religion of Christ and now worships the idols of Hindu tradition.

In fact, he has a room in his house which no visitor, least of all a fellow Englishman or woman or European, can enter. Only he and select servants of the household, intimates and those who have brought about or encouraged this shame, share the secret.

The room is rumoured to have an idol or several in the corner, graven images before which the sahib-gone-native prostrates himself in shameful and pagan ceremonies. The whisper in the club says that he worships an idol, a 'joss'.

The contemptuous word is no more than an anglicized

distortion of Dios, the Portuguese word for God. The Latin root is Deus, the Greek pagan version being Zeus and the Indo-Anglian parallel in Sanskrit is Dev, rendered in Marathi and other offshoot languages as Deo. Most religious traditions, except the very puritanical or fundamentalist, allow the burning of incense as a fumigating or purifying agent of the atmosphere of a place of worship or shrine. Some denominations light candles as offerings. Hindu Gods, symbolized in statuesque form, have incense lit before them to sweeten the air. The incense, turned into convenient sticks that burn over an interval of time and spread their perfume, are then known as joss-sticks, sticks offered before or to Dios.

VERBAL CRUSADES

All over the world people invent rude names, epithets and even rhymes for people of other faiths, sects or religions. The Ulster Protestants call the Catholics 'left-footers' and worse.

The Parsis, for some reason, were branded 'crow-eaters' and I remember the parodic verse I heard in school:

Parsi, Parsi kagra khao
Mamma bola biscuit lao
Ek biscuit kachcha
Mama key peyt mey bachcha'

(Parsi, Parsi eater of crows
'Fetch me a biscuit,' mummy goes
One biscuit is not quite done
Mummy's oven is sporting a bun!)

Some terms for other religions were meant to be merely descriptive but suffered from the precepts and perceptions of their times. The first European writers to write about the Muslims called them Mahometans, or followers of

Mahomet – their rendition of the Prophet Muhammad. This was in analogy to the followers of Christ being called Christians in ignorance of the fact that the latter follow him as God made flesh, while Muslims are not followers of the Prophet Muhammad who was merely a messenger of God and enjoined humanity to worship him. Muslims don't name themselves followers of Muhammad, but want to be known as those who subjugate themselves in obeisance to the Supreme Being.

In reverse, Indian Muslims call the Christians 'Issahi' or followers of 'Issah', which is with Yeshua the equivalent of Jesus. They avoid the Christ word because they believe that Jesus was not the son of God and, therefore, part of his substance, but a human and a prophet with a message from God.

Any number of texts, in English, Portuguese and Dutch in the sixteenth and succeeding centuries, alluded to the Hindu population of India as 'ghentus' – from the Portuguese word for gentiles or people who were not of the true faith, which to them was Christianity. The division into the 'us and them' categories with gentiles being classed as 'them' originated with the Jews who referred to non-Jews, including Christians, as 'gentiles'.

THE ACCENT FALLS

The rule of the consonant shift in English dictates that when a syllable is added to a word as an additional suffix, the accent in the pronunciation of the word moves further to the right. So 'family' is spoken with the emphasis on 'fam'; 'familiar', with the added suffix is accented on 'mil'; familiarity is, with the shift, accented on the syllable 'iar'.

The English break the rule of their own language when it comes to the nomenclature of the great mountain range that bounds northern Indian. Hindustanis call the mountains the Himalayas, the abode of snows, and the word is pronounced with the emphasis on the first syllable 'him'. There is no 'lay' in Himalayas! The English may have thought the name of the range was arrived at by the addition of syllables to the word 'him', and thus, using the consonant shift, they placed the emphasis on the third syllable: 'lay'. This would be playing according to the rule if the name had been built by 'Him' turning to 'Hima' and to 'Himalay' and then Himalayas. But it wasn't. It was a proper noun when the Brits first heard it.

And why do they say Pathan, sounding and rhyming it like

Satan rather than with 'pa' as in pathetic and 'than' to rhyme with barn or tarn?

Then there are the Gurkhas who have garnered a lot of sympathy as mercenaries for the Crown denied their proper pensions and residence permits in Britain. Yes, sure, feel sorry for them and support their political rights, but stop pronouncing it to rhyme with 'jerkers'. The first of the two syllables, 'Gur', actually rhymes with 'sur', as in surreal, and the second syllable is 'khas' – the vowel pronounced exactly as in 'cars' and the 'kh' being as it is spelt – a 'k' accompanied, rather than followed, by the 'h' in a short exhalation against the palate.

Pronunciation is never a matter of life and death except, perhaps, with the shibboleth test of Jewishness by which your correct pronunciation of particular formulations proved that you were of the faith and excused you from execution. In a globalized world, pronunciation should, when taken into a different culture, retain some authenticity but I don't think one can say that to Americans or Australians.

In India, the word 'mobile', as in 'mobile phone', is pronounced with the emphasis on the second syllable, the 'bile' being dominant.

So also 'adult', which is in India pronounced 'er-dult', with an emphasized 'dult' to rhyme with cult; so also adolescent with the emphasis on 'dol'.

When Peter Brook, the celebrated theatre director, adopted the Mahabharata as a project to turn into nine hours of drama, the name of the Indian epic became popular in England and the West. Only, it was pronounced with wrong syllables emphasized.

The correct emphasis is a dual one with stresses on the first syllable 'Mah', and a slightly stronger one on 'bha', with the 'ra' and 'ta' being skipped over lightly. It emerges as Màhh-bhà-rutha. The English distortion is placing the emphasis on the 'ra' and elevating its sound to 'raa' as though it were part of a hurrah! So it's pronounced 'ma-brr-raà-ter'.

SEVEN ISLANDS

The origin of the name of Bombay is disputed. The seven islands off the western coast have been inhabited since the Stone Age. There is evidence that Emperor Ashoka of the third-century Maurya dynasty, who proclaimed Buddhism as the state religion of India, established the islands as part of his empire. The islands passed through the hands of several dynasties of western India and in the fourteenth century came under the rule of the Mughal governors of Gujarat, who rented the islands by treaty to Portuguese traders in the sixteenth.

The Portuguese didn't want to develop or inhabit the islands, but they found the strip of water between the islands and the mainland the best natural harbour, sheltered from the storms of the monsoon, on the entire west coast of India. It is claimed they referred to their acquisition as 'bom baia'.

The British acquired the islands in the seventeenth century as a dowry for Katherine of Braganza who married Charles II of England. The transfer of the islands as part of the dowry didn't allude to a city called Bombay because there wasn't one. The East India Company began building such a city by draining and reclaiming the swamps between the islands.

It began, under British times, to be called Bombay, as the British took over the name from the Portuguese. The problem with this derivation is that 'baia' doesn't mean harbour. It means beach, and the inlet used as a harbour is not in any geographical sense a beach. In fact, quite the opposite. It is a deep enough finger of water between the islands and the mainland to allow larger ships to enter and dock.

There is the other favoured story about the origin of the city's name. Within the city there are territories named after religious landmarks. There is, to the south, Kalbadevi, which is named after the temple to the goddess Kali. Further up the island is the district called Prabhadevi, probably named after a temple built by a goldsmith philanthropist called Prabhu.

Between Byculla and the north-west on the Harbour Branch local railway line lies the area known as Pydhoni – a word composed of the Marathi for 'py', which means feet, and 'dhoni', which means to wash. This may simply allude to the fact that there was shallow water between sections of land across which one could wade, or it may mean a ceremonial washing of the feet in the water of the creek.

The current name for the city, Mumbai, is derived from the temple of Mumba Devi. The first term is a conglomerate of Maha Amba, Great Mother. The second term is simply 'goddess'. The temple dating from the sixteenth century dedicated to Mumba Devi still stands in south Mumbai and is a functional temple, but the story goes that the worship of Maha Amba and shrines and temples to her, go back deep in history from the earliest inhabitation of the islands as she is the deity of the Agri, the salt-making tribes, and the Kolis, the fishermen.

The new name, Mumbai, is seen by some as an imposition of a Hindu name for a multi-religious city. The name was officially changed by a coalition in which the Shiv Sena, very much a self-confessed Hindu chauvinist party, was the dominant partner. It was a democratic decision, in the way of Indian democracy, and hanging on to the name Bombay, as some rear-guardists insist, is a lost cause.

There are cities all over the world called Saint this or that, despite the fact that Jews, Muslims or atheists form part of the population. So also in India there are cities named after the practice and beliefs of Islam, for instance 'Allahabad', the abode of God.

THE SPELL

In Hindustan one grows up with superstition. In my childhood there were serious cases of criminal deviations caused by it. The newspapers at the time reported that the police were investigating the disappearance of a child who they believed had been sacrificed at the building site of a bridge because the gods of the waters, who allowed the bridging of rivers, were thirsty for human infant blood.

There were also scary stories, spread in a rumour that actually gripped the whole town, of a spirit called the 'hakmaribai' who had the body of a crow and the head of a hag. She was reputed to fly close to your window or your street and call out for help in the voice of someone dear to you. When you answered the call, she would kill you and eat your guts. Over the few weeks that the rumour prevailed, I must have heard the story from several people, who swore they had been close to the victims or had even heard her call in their neighbourhood.

One of the aunts in whose house I grew up insisted that she believed in God and not in any superstitions, but just in case I did encounter any demonic avatars, I was to repeat the incantation 'shikastey shikastey sheytaan' three times and then start saying my Zoroastrian prayers. It was a guaranteed protection against all evil.

It was my aunt's personal 'mantra'. In Hindu mythology, a mantra is used to conjure up good, summon the gods, the supernatural, to ask for protection, to command a magic weapon and for a myriad other purposes. The word has passed into English and is now used to mean something that is repeated over and over again. It generally carries the connotation of some oft-repeated truism which does not meet with the speaker's approval: 'Obama repeats his mantra of "yes we can", but over two terms he's demonstrated that he can't!'

BEARING UP

If you carried a cup for a king you were the cup-bearer. If you carried a body to its grave, you were a pallbearer. The bearers of bad tidings, in the tradition of punishing the messenger, have often suffered.

There is the other meaning of 'bearing' which originates from the tortures of Tantalus, the one who absorbs, accommodates and tolerates pain.

If you serve at table as a waiter in a restaurant in India, high or low, seven star or no star, you may be addressed as 'behrar'. The word has even been distorted into 'bahirah' and is used for any variety of table or kitchen attendant.

The designation obviously arose in fanciful Raj days. In *The Smith Administration*, the series of stories by Kipling about a Mr Smith and his establishment of Indian servants, there are 'coachwans', the drivers of coaches, 'dhobis', the washermen, khansamas, the chefs, and twenty others. Among them, the 'bearers'.

The Brits brought the word to India but didn't carry it back. In most Indian establishments such as clubs and restaurants or even in servant-employing households, 'call the bearer' would be understood. In Britain, they would wonder which mythology you stepped out of.

Other words made the journey to India but didn't return. A classic example is 'thrice'. The British would now say 'once', 'twice' and 'three times'.

In south India, I have heard black coffee referred to as 'decoction'. It wouldn't be understood in Starbucks or Costa in London, dictionary English though it is – and certainly would be legitimate on a Scrabble board.

PARIAHS

The campaigns against smoking and the bans imposed by law on doing it in public places have forced the hungry-lungers to take to the pavements and porches of cities. My guests, though no one in the house objects to smoking, religiously ask to be let out into the cold to sneak a fag. That's putting it as I see it, though others would call it 'indulging their nasty, selfish addiction'.

The status of smokers as outcastes is supposedly new. In the middle decades of the last century, it was considered stylish and part of a modish maturity. And yet this is not the first time that smoking and smokers are held in some contempt. In 1842, William Makepeace Thackeray writes in *The Fitz-Boodle Papers*: 'What is this smoking that it should be considered a crime? I believe in my heart that women are jealous of it, as of a rival. They speak of it as of some secret, awful vice that seizes upon a man, and makes him a pariah from genteel society.'

The word he uses is 'pariah'. Mark Twain after him uses the same word in characterizing Huckleberry Finn's status.

So in English, from the early seventeenth century and the

journals of the British in India, the word has come to mean 'outcaste'.

In my boyhood, as today, stray dogs roamed the streets of Indian cities. We used to refer to them as 'pahdiahs' and I always assumed that the name derived from the 'pahad' or mountain, associating the stray dogs of the city to the wild dogs and wolves of the mountains. That derivation didn't contain the contamination of caste which the word, in English, has acquired. The 'mountainous' derivation is probably inaccurate but understandable as it is analogous to calling a wild person a 'junglee', a forest dweller. The word 'forest', of course, is a benign collection of trees and the worst it offers is Robin Hood and his merry men. A jungle, on the other hand, a word from Sanskrit and then Hindustani, denotes deep and dense vegetation, full of darkness and danger.

The favoured derivation of pariah is from the Tamil 'paraiyar', the word for the low-caste drummers of Hindu kings who acted as street-criers, playing a drum for attention and making the announcements the regime wanted disseminated. The men who performed these functions were considered to be in the periphery of society. The earliest British settlements in India came into contact with Tamil kingdoms and the word worked its way into their usage.

BUCKET FOOD

In the sixties and seventies, the East Pakistani – later Bangladeshi – immigrant settlement brought an Indian restaurant to most high streets that would permit one to set up. It was a great boon to late-evening drinkers whose taste for a curry after a hard night's drinking was often expressed in the ambivalent 'I could murder an Indian!'

The Bangladeshi restaurant was a sort of revenge for colonialism, and instead of being called Star of India or The Taj Mahal or even, quite mysteriously, The Light of Gurkha, they should all have been called 'The Empire Strikes Back'.

They made what we call 'papads' in western India famous as 'popadoms'. The British won't recognize the former word and so even Gujarati or Punjabi restaurants have to advertise the crispy accompaniment as popadoms.

The British Bangladeshi high street restaurant also established the convention that Indian food was a test of endurance and an Indian meal could deteriorate into a competition between drunkards to see who could tolerate the dish with the most chilli content. English has, unlike Hindustani which has the convenient words 'jhaal' and 'garam', no two words to distinguish between the chilli-hot and the temperature-hot. Both are 'hot'.

The competition for chilli-hotness has induced some Indian restaurants to grade their offerings into mild, medium and hot categories and give them exotic names such as 'Chicken Malaya', 'Chicken Korma', 'Chicken Dupiazza', 'Chicken Madras' and 'Chicken Vindaloo' so that the clients can feel they are familiar with the grades of discomfort afforded by this ascending order. That it has nothing to do with the way Granny or the chefs of India used to serve it, bothers nobody.

In the eighties, the restaurants of Birmingham came up with an innovation in menu. These were not Bangladeshi restaurants but Pakistani ones with more authentic northern Pakistani food. They were by and large owned by Mirpuris from what is known as 'Azad Kashmir', to Pakistan and 'Pak Occupied Kashmir (POK)', to India. These restaurants introduced a category on their menu known as 'balti', offering balti chicken, balti lamb, balti keema, etc. The trend caught on and several restaurants named themselves Balti restaurants.

Balti, the restaurants claim, is the name of the Wok-shaped pot in which the food was cooked. Now, it is possible that in some part of Mirpur the cooking dish the rest of the subcontinent calls a 'kadhai' is known as a balti. To the rest of India and Pakistan, a balti is a bucket, the sort you carry water to bathe in. It would be an absurdity in, say, Mumbai to cook anything in a 'balti'.

The alternative explanation, but not a very popular or recognized one, occurred to me through a memory of a scene in Kipling's *Kim*. The boy, Kim, travels with the Red Lama to

Mehboob Ali's camp in the north and their host invites him to eat but tells the Lama, who won't eat food at a Muslim's table, to go and find the stable boys, his 'baltis', and share their meal. These stable boys are so called because they are from the region of the very north of Pakistan called Baltistan. It made me wonder whether the tradition of Balti cuisine had come to Birmingham and the rest of Britain through the agency of Mirpuris who know not what they dispense.

OOPS!

The word 'Sindh' for the province to the east of Baluchistan and south of the Punjab comes from the ancient Persian 'Indos', or the Sanskrit 'Sindhu', for the river Indus. We know the river by this last name because it's what the Greeks, taking their cue from the Persian Empire to their east, called it. The land of the Indus, at the west of which Alexander's armies stopped, was dubbed India and the natives, sticking to the Sanskrit derivation, called it Sindh.

The name of the king that Alexander defeated in the provinces west of the Indus has come down to us through Greek historians and legend as 'Porus'. Indian historians have speculatively claimed that the name was just a mistaken derivation from the word 'purush', meaning 'man' in Sanskrit. It is a historical fact that the provinces of Baluchistan and Sindh at the time (326 BC and on) when Alexander and his raider army invaded, were satrapies of the Persian Empire of Darius III. The name 'Porus' is a common Zoroastrian Parsi name from ancient Persia and is not a Hindu or Sanskrit name at all.

The territory of Sindh passed into Pakistan in August

1947. Yet the Indian national anthem contains, in its list which defines India, the province or state of Sindh. This is because the national anthem was composed by Rabindranath Tagore before he knew of the possibility of the partition of India. It has remained in the national anthem, not because nobody noticed, but because it would have been an act of vandalism to Bowdlerize Tagore's verses and, perhaps, in recognition of the fact that the Hindu Sindhi population which either lived in India before Partition or came as refugees after it, are very much part of democratic India. And yet the anomaly remains in India's national anthem.

A friend of mine wrote a biography of a very prominent Indian politician. Though Indian in origin, this author is British and is not a native Hindi or Urdu speaker. In translating a document from Hindi in the text of the biography, the author made the howling mistake of rendering the phrase 'aam junta', or the common man, as 'the mango people' because the word aam also means 'mango'. A mischievous relative of the politician who no doubt read the book carefully used the howler in a tweet calling his critics 'the mango people of the banana republic'.

One of the great speeches of the twentieth century, in the same rank, perhaps, as those of Churchill and Martin Luther King, is the speech India's first prime minister, Pandit

Jawaharlal Nehru delivered on the fifteenth of August 1947, in the hour of India's Independence. He began the momentous speech using the famous phrase in his introductory remarks: 'Long years ago, we made a tryst with destiny, and now the time comes when we shall redeem our pledge, not wholly or in full measure, but very substantially. At the stroke of the midnight hour, when the world sleeps, India will awake to life and freedom.'

Now, Panditji, a seasoned traveller, was certainly aware of time zones and of the fact that at the stroke of midnight in India, it would be daylight on the American continent and twilight in England and Africa. The 'world' was certainly not literally asleep. Even metaphorically, one would have thought that the moment of decolonization of India would have commanded the attention of the world public. Perhaps Panditji thought that the rhetorical impact of the phrase outweighed any literal nitpicking.

SUBLIME TO RIDICULOUS

In my childhood, one of the spells one intoned while playing at magic or at conjuring tricks was adopted from Disney's Cinderella:

Salakadoola
Menchikaboola
Bibbety Bobbety Boo.

As yet supercalifragilisticexpialidocious had not been invented.

Local street magicians used other spells and incantations. A man would make coloured balls disappear from under a handkerchief after waving his fingers and a wand to the rhythm of 'Begi begi and jill jilly!' Then there was, of course, 'open sesame' and there was the universal 'abracadabra'.

Another magic spell, usually associated with an act of disappearance, was the word 'aflatoon', as in waving one's fingers and performing the vanishing trick by saying 'Aflatoon chhoo ho jao!' – Aflatoon, disappear!

It wasn't till years and the absorption of a lot of useful and useless information that I realized that the magic word was actually the name Arab scholars had, through their contact with classical learning, used for Plato.

How the name of the father of classical philosophy and ethics came to be degraded to a magic spell to make marbles disappear, is a mystery. Or perhaps not. The works of Plato may have, for centuries, been difficult and even appeared as mysterious to the ignorant or to those with very different cultural assumptions. We do say 'it's all Greek to me!'

Perhaps the mystery was expressed or conceived as 'it's all Aflatoon to me', and then the name of the king of mysteries was invoked to perform that which defied the laws of nature.

PLUNDER

One of my favourite light qawwalis begins:

'Hummey tho loot liya milkey
Husn waalon ney
Kaley kaley baalon ney
Gorey gorey gaalon ney!'

(My heart has been stolen
By the beauty of this pair
Her fair complexion,
Her jet-black hair.)

The one word that needs no translation is 'loot'. It comes
to English through Anglo-Indian contact and is derived
from the similarly pronounced Hindustani word which
originally meant 'plunder'. The word itself came from the
Sanskrit 'lunt' with a nasal sound where the consonant 'n'
is. That too meant wealth taken from an enemy or by force.
The derivatives in Hindustani such as 'lootera', the looter,

retain the meaning of violent acquisition while also being susceptible to the gentler metaphorical meaning as in the qawwali. In English it has come to mean, apart from snatched wealth, any collection of it.

SETTLED

The word 'camp' has travelled some distance. One contemporary joke acknowledges the change in meaning by describing the behaviour or mannerism of a male as being 'camp as row of tents!'

I grew up in a part of Poona town which had two names, one which emanates from its canvas settlement origins. A letter to the house and street where we lived in could be addressed either to 'Poona Cantonment' or 'Poona Camp'. It would have, despite the vagaries of the Indian postal services, an equal chance of getting to its destination.

Poona Camp, today Pune Camp, is distinct from the area of the same town called City. That the City should exist within a town, or within the larger concept of Poona City, is not entirely unique. The commercial district of London is called The City of London whereas the whole of London can equally validly be referred to as the city. The part has the same name as the whole.

Our segment of Poona/Pune got its name from the British East India Company's army camping there on either side of the Mula-Mutha rivers in 1817. The camps, rapidly expanding with new regiments being settled in it, was soon transformed from canvas to brick, and stone with roads navigable by horse and cart.

Elsewhere in India, such complexes were christened after the Chinese word 'canton' for a settlement and the army sector of towns began to be known as cantonments.

ONE MAN'S MEAT

School children in Britain use the word 'mong' as a form of abuse. They use it without compunction in order to call each other fools or idiots, and I soon discovered that it was short from 'mongoloid', the word that characterized people with Down's syndrome.

This reprehensible term originated from a supposed characterization of the features of these sufferers as resembling the races of north-eastern Asia, the Mongols.

The name of these races has, in India, and now through transference to English, far from being a term of abuse, come to be a mark of power, distinction and wealth. The word Mogol, rendered as Mughal, was the name of the grand dynasty of Zair-ud-din Babur whose rule in Delhi from 1526 gave rise to a dynasty which lasted with some power into the eighteenth century and then, with diminished power and titular status, into the nineteenth, till 1858.

Babur claimed descent from Timur-e-lang ('the lame Timur', whose description as one-legged turned into the Western name of the ruthless conqueror: Tamerlane). He also listed Ghenghis Khan as his ancestor and both being Mongols, his race was characterized by the populace of India as 'Mogol'. The word transferred to English as a personage with power, a controller as in 'Hollywood Mogul'.

FAR FROM SIMPLE

A young lady friend, part of our company as we sat down to dinner in a fancy restaurant in New Delhi, chose an injudicious moment to tell us how she had been to another rather expensive restaurant and had picked up food poisoning. She should have terminated the anecdote at that point but she merrily went on to give the company the details of what she had suffered. She said that for the next few hours of the evening and night she was 'simply voiding'.

I don't think the British segment of our six-strong table understood quite what she meant, but the Indians got the drift. I think the verb 'to void' didn't come across and the adverb, though correctly used, is now a peculiarly Indian and even south Indian usage for having contracted loose motions.

The word 'simply' has in India acquired the connotation of something extreme.

A Tamil friend at college would express a strong affirmative with the adverbial assertion. 'So despite the notices, did he commit a nuisance?' The answer, with an outward wave of the palm for emphasis, would be, 'Simply!' – meaning yes, he did!

The word hasn't changed its function or meaning. In English usage, when it was largely used, it could mean 'to the extremes'. In India, it is rarely used to mean in a straightforward and plain manner as in: 'a simply worded sentence'. It would be used as in: 'For four days it was simply raining.'

OFFICIAL GRAFFITI

I have seen posters, in India, on shop fronts and walls which say 'Post no bills'. No self-reference there? It should, of course, have been 'Post no other bills'.

There are still notices on the walls lining Indian streets which say 'Commit no nusiance'. To any international reader of English, this would probably mean 'don't indulge in any behaviour that would be anti-social', or 'don't sing or shout too loudly or grimace at passers-by'. To Indians, it doesn't mean that. It's an injunction to refrain from pissing against the particular wall.

In some instances, perhaps for the benefit of those who didn't read English or any other language, the notice has been replaced with tiles depicting Hindu Gods or even a few words in Arabic from the Koran. This would, it is hoped, inhibit people from committing a nuisance, defiling the sacred and bringing down the wrath of the gods or God on them.

THE 'H' WORD

One of the members of our film crew on a trip to India was a West Indian friend called Darcus. We travelled from London to New Delhi.

Darcus is a black Trinidadian. We had been together in the immigrant, or black, politics of Britain for the best part of thirty years and in the course of that, strictly between ourselves, he picked up the word 'Hubshi', which Indians use as a rude tag for black people. The word was thrown about in our circle as a group of American blacks might refer to each other in defiant playfulness as 'nigger' while not tolerating the use of the offensive term by anyone else.

Darcus was immediately impressed by the grandeur of the capital as we drove through it on the way in. He looked around.

'Dhondy, who built all this?' he asked.

'The Brits,' I said

'They intended to stay, boy,' he remarked.

A few evenings later, as the preparations for the shoot progressed, the producer of *Bandit Queen* took us to the Delhi Gymkhana, another ex-Raj institution and building. Before dinner, we were escorted into the bar, which was crowded that evening with the great and grand of Delhi, from government officials, the elite of the judiciary to high-ranking professionals of the city, their families and guests.

Darcus was impressed by the façade and the dance floor as we entered, and then as we walked into the air-conditioned lounge bar, stood a few steps in and looking around said, loudly enough for the room to hear, 'Check this, man! The old Hubshi has arrived.'

It was as though there had been a small explosion at the door. The bar felt silent as they heard the 'H' word and took in the fact that it was a black man calling himself a Hubshi. Our host bought the drinks and a couple of gentlemen approached Darcus and engaged him in welcoming conversation. One of them had been India's ambassador in the West Indies, recognized the accent and came over to make Darcus feel at home and swap nostalgia. That the rest of the people in the bar had heard him was mildly embarrassing as some came and asked our host who he was and why was he using that sort of language? A desire to shock? A joke?

A mistaken valuation of the word would be the correct answer. The word, used derogatorily in India, comes from the Arab word 'Habasah', which in turn comes from the syllable 'hbsh' in the Aramaic, the language Jesus spoke. The Arabs have long characterized the land of the north-west of Africa as the country of Christians, Muslims and Jews, the 'mixed' tribes and religions of the region. The word 'hbsh' originally meant 'diverse'.

The word gave its name to the region and became, in English, Abyssinia. Indians characterized all Africans as Abyssinians and called them Hubshis, which came to mean

black people, and acquired derogatory connotations. In the
Mumbai bazaars, one can buy plantains for frying or boiling,
a fruit that can't be eaten raw. They are called 'hubshi kela'
– 'Negro bananas' – or more popularly now 'Madrasi kela',
because they come from the coasts of the south.

GYMKHANA

In Poona there was a decrepit building in the cantonment area off Kahun Road called the Parsi Gymkhana. Kahun Road was signposted as such but was always referred to as 'Khan' Road, the sign being a misspelling or the Mr Kahun who gave it its name, having passed into mysterious oblivion.

The Gymkhana had a swimming pool with dark-green waters that were home to frogs, a fact that didn't deter my friends and I from swimming there at 6.30 in the morning before school in the hot season. The building had an L-shaped veranda with card tables at which old Parsi gentlemen sat in foursomes throughout the year, losing money to each other in three-card flush, poker or rummy games.

There may have been badminton and tennis courts, but they were never used. It was a dreary place, and apart from the swimmers was, according to my grandfather, a refuge for desperate gamblers.

My friend and neighbour's father was a regular one of these. He would bicycle off in the mid-morning to the Gymkhana and return in the evening, downcast at having lost or jubilant at having won some money. When he lost, he would spend the next few days away from the Gymkhana, sitting on the doorstep of his house in a chair overlooking the street, reading brown-paper-covered pornographic books and jiggling his knees in rhythmic excitement as he read. For my grandfather, this neighbour's routines were enough to confirm his prejudices about the character of Parsi Gymkhana regulars.

There was no equestrian pastime at the Gymkhana, though the word in Britain has come to mean a horse-show of one sort or the other. In India, it means anything from a smart sporting club, to an exercise salon or, indeed, an ex-Raj exclusive club for self-selecting members.

In the early twentieth century, Lord Willingdon, the Governor of Bombay, attempted to take his Indian guests to the Bombay Gymkhana. His guests were refused admission on racial grounds. He was powerless to defy or change the rules of the Gymkhana and instead, in a liberal rage, is reputed to have founded the rival Willingdon Club, which was proud to be multiracial.

These Gymkhanas have cricket pitches and teams and facilities for all manner of sports and rooms for members of affiliated clubs and members' guests to stay.

The word is reputed to be an amalgam of 'gym' from the Greek for exercise and 'khana' from Hindustani, meaning a room or an enclosure.

WORKSHY

Our history books referred to the high officials in the East India Company at the time of Robert Clive as 'factors'. These factors set up and administered 'factories'. As post-manufacturing-capitalist generations this usage seemed a bit archaic. Surely a factory was where things were made and not a place where trading goods were stored? And a factor was something not from a history but a mathematical lesson, in which a factor was a number which divided into another?

Even so, I accepted that English moved in mysterious ways its felicities to accomplish!

Then in the sixties, when the thinking younger generations of the West became rebellious and left-leaning and declared themselves Marxists, Leninist, Bolsheviks and Maoists of several orders, there came the need for communal discussion, formulation and resolution. The groupuscules that were formed and the conferences that were called on most questions, and with very many agendas, evolved a discussion mode, which they dubbed a 'workshop'.

The term became widespread and began to be applied to any collection of people dedicated to some task of exploration of a subject. It even began to apply, in my professional experience, to the improvisation of comedy formats. I was, in the early eighties, a member of a theatrical group called the Black Theatre Co-operative. A TV producer, on seeing our stage work, proposed that we, writers, actors and a director get together in a 'workshop' and come up with a proposal for a TV sitcom. We did.

We worked at the ideas and improvisations and it was a productive formatting forum. I suppose 'workshop' was a convenient enough name for the collective activity, but it felt a bit of a cheat because it didn't entail blood, sweat or tears and the word had acquired, for us lefties, the connotations of the dark, satanic mills of industry.

The word was borrowed from industry in order that the chatterers and intellectuals who formed the 'workshops' could feel they were engaged in activity which emulated the proletariat. Physical work was considered more ennobling and certainly in the sixties, when the word was born, the intellectuals wanted to pass themselves off as 'workers'.

THE NAME OF THE LETTER

In one logical aside, Bertrand Russell explains why the name of a number is not the number. The understanding proved why certain riddles work – for instance, the childish trick we used to play of counting our fingers backwards as in 'ten, nine, eight, seven, six' for the fingers of one hand and then brandishing the fingers of the other hand adding 'six and five', seemingly adding up to the impossible eleven. I don't think anyone was fooled, but few could explain why the numbering trick didn't work. Russell's explanation applies. Counting forwards you name your fingers 'one, two, three ... etc.' It seems okay then to call the last counted finger 'ten' and then the next one 'nine' and the subsequent ones 'eight, 'seven' and 'six'. These are not the numbers, they are the names we gave to the fingers we used to count the numbers.

The use of the name of the letter 'S' and its corruptions as a substitute for its sound in some Indian pronunciation is noticeable and has been noted by writers. A friend's e-mail address contains the word 'ishtyle' in a parody or literal representation of some Indian pronunciation of the word 'style'.

Another friend insists that her cook is serving up a traditional north Indian Muslim dish called 'ishtoo'. She resists the notion that it's an Indian khansama's way of saying 'stew'.

In Forster's *A Passage to India*, at a climactic point in the action, the Indian crowds gather outside a courtroom chanting the mantra 'Esmiss Esmoor!' They are calling upon the old English colonial lady who has taken their side – Mrs Moore.

Forster was not the first to note and use this quirk.

In Rudyard Kipling's stories collected as *The Smith Administration*, the official who commands his retinue of the servants in his employ who live in the servants' quarters within his compound address him 'Eschmitt Sahib'.

My grandmother's generation, referring to someone as not being quite mentally sound would say, touching their temples with their fingers and adopting two English words in the Gujarati phrase: 'ehnoo iskoroon loose chhe' – he has a screw loose!

FUNDAMENTALLY

A north Indian usage which I always thought was authentically Urdu is nothing of the sort. Friends used to ask one to get to the root of the matter with the phrase 'funda kya hai, yaar?' Meaning, 'what's the funda'.

I realized it was an abbreviation for the English 'fundamental' only when a popular British Asian band called and advertised itself as 'Fun-da-mental'. They were inspired by the anarchy and rebellion of the British punk generation of pop and used the Indian slang for basics, though there may have been a mischievous allusion, being an Asian band, to fundamentalist tendencies.

The plural most used in India is 'fundas'. The abbreviation means nothing to the British and is an example of an abbreviated word from one language passing into another and taking root with its own special meaning.

PUPPY SHOW

'What are you staring at? This is not a puppy show!' or words to that effect were used in my childhood to challenge unwelcome on-lookers. I can only guess that litters of puppies, born to the memsahib's household, would have been on display to those who were invited to view and adopt them. Or there may have been dog shows or public shows of puppies in which all and sundry were welcome.

Denying an event, a phenomenon or a scene the status of a 'puppy show' was an assertion that it was private.

CLOSE THE LIGHT

In an interview on television, Benazir Bhutto recalled the first time that assassins made an attempt on her life. She had just become prime minister of Pakistan, replacing General Musharraf through some internationally, mainly American-brokered deal. The second attempt succeeded and Benazir died, reportedly of bullet wounds, though a theory perpetrated by rumour is that she died of concussion having banged her head into the back of the armoured car in which she was standing to acknowledge the cheers of the crowd.

In the interview, she said that as her cavalcade progressed through the streets, the lights went out.

'They were closing the lights,' she said. 'Why were they closing the lights?'

Othello said, 'put out the light' and the advent of electricity and switches has given us 'switch the lights off'. One extinguishes flames and that can be construed as putting out the light. To 'close' the light is, of course, a literal translation of '*batti band karo*' from Urdu or other Indian languages.

When we, as teenagers, listened to our records, no doubt making an unbearable racket with Elvis Presley, Mukesh, Lata,

194

The Kingston Trio and the now long forgotten Bobby Darin, my grandfather would come in from the veranda where he sat on most days diligently assembling his stamp collection. He'd put his hands on his ears and say '*Jara slow karo. Ghanoo loud vagaaroch. Slow karo!*' (Turn it down. It's much too loud. Turn the volume down.) He might gesture with his fingers to indicate the turning of the amplifier's knob. He confounded soft with slow because he was translating the word 'halloo', which could mean either.

PEARLS

As I grow older, several friends and relatives, though not as yet myself, develop 'cataracts' in their eyes – the misting over of the eye's lenses. The latest procedure involves the shattering of the affected lens before replacing it with an artificial one all in the course of fifteen minutes. The patient walks away in the same half-hour sans cataract.

It's curious that the same word in English means a waterfall. The connection is probably metaphorical, of a thickness that cascades over the optic lens.

In Gujarati, the word for the increasingly opaque covering of the lens is 'motyo' or 'pearl', which is, of course, a description of the white beady appearance of the affected lens.

The simile, though not current in English, may have occurred to Shakespeare when in *The Tempest* he writes:

'Those are pearls that were his eyes:
Nothing of him that doth fade
But doth suffer a sea-change...'

CHANCE

One way of greeting the desirable, but impossible, in English is to say, 'Chance would be a fine thing!' It's saying, 'I can wish it would happen but it won't.' So, if someone said to me on the Internet, for example that I was about to win millions of dollars in the Nigerian lottery, I might say, 'Chance would be a fine thing!' – or I might contact the cyber-police!

In my college days in India, the word 'chance' had acquired the connotation of accessibility to romance. So if one saw, in the corridors or grounds of the college, a boy speaking to a girl, it would be assumed that he was trying to chat her up, and the rowdy elements of the fraternity would shout 'chance hai!'

The concept was expanded by turning the noun into an Anglo-hybrid verb with a Hindustani suffix as in 'chance-marraoing'. It meant he was attempting to attract her romantic attention.

BUTTERING UP

The construction of verbs from Indian nouns was not uncommon. To attempt to flatter or to insinuate oneself into someone's favour is commonly known in English as 'buttering up'. This is translated, using the Bombay-idiom word for butter, into 'maska-lagaoing'. It literally means 'putting on the butter', and is the very active metaphor for flattery.

PARLEZ VOUS

Before I knew what French was, I used to hear my father and his friends, mostly co-officers in the British-Indian and then in the Indian army singing a strange song on the picnics to which we were taken from army settlements.

Considering that all these officers had been through the Second World War, fighting the Japanese in Burma or the Andaman Islands or encountering the Germans in Africa or Mesopotamia, it was, now in hindsight, a rather irreverent ditty about the Germans invading France. In this Indian army version it went:

> *The German soldiers crossed the line*
> *Parlez Vous!*
> *The German soldiers crossed the line*
> *Parlez vous?*
> *The German soldiers crossed the line*
> *To kiss the women and drink the wine*
> *Inky-pinky-parlez vous!'*

The French is, of course, doggerel invented by someone

in the British army. I now know that my dad and the other officers, singing the song in front of women and children, substituted 'kiss' as a euphemism for what the British troops sang.

What is mildly surprising is that the song seems to rejoice in the humiliation of the British ally, France, by the German enemy. It's probably a manifestation of the jokey contempt that the British have or feign for the French as in, 'How many Frenchmen does it take to defend Paris?' – answer: 'Don't know, it's never been tried.'

There were other sanitized songs on these picnics. The picnickers would sing '*She'll be coming round the mountain when she comes*,' whose verses get bawdier and more risque as the circle is invited to invent the next verse. One celebrated verse, mild in the context of today was, 'She'll be wearing no pyjamas when she comes,' but this was always modified to 'wearing pink pyjamas' to spare the blushes of the Indian ladies and the sensibilities of the children who, like myself, knew from the knowing smirks on the men's faces that this was a euphemism for nakedness.

But back to the French, and allow me a slight diversion: people from Trinidad often use the phrase 'it have' for 'there is', as in, 'it have a duppy in dat house on de hill'. Trinidad used to be a French colony before it was British and the French phrase 'il y a' was then literally translated into English and 'there is' became 'it have'.

India, apart from the port of Pondicherry, was never colonized by the French but in two words that I can think of lies evidence that their language did penetrate Indian languages. The word 'savon' for soap is rendered as 'saabun' in Hindustani and Gujarati.

However, the word for spring in Hindi is 'saavan' and is certainly celebrated in folklore as the season of fresh winds and cleanliness. Could it be that soap was first called 'savan' in a metmetaphor for this cleanliness and then passed into the French?

And the other word? The Urdu or Hindustani word for a church is 'kalisa', but I think this comes from the Christian influence on the Middle East from which the Arabs picked up the word 'eglise', transformed and adopted it.

JUNGLEES

A society which was divided into castes and hierarchies of caste will naturally evolve derogatory terms for people considered of a lower caste. There are scores of words in common use in Hindustani for castes whose function as scavengers, as people who skin animals and tan leather, or those whose job is to deal with human excreta, which have passed into the language as general abuse. The words 'chamar' or 'bhangi', beginning as distinctions of trade are, today, in a society whose ideal is democracy, terms of abuse.

There are other, possibly less derogatory or abusive terms. In demotic Hindustani and also in the Gujarati my Parsi community speaks, the word 'junglee' is applied to an uncultivated, uncouth, ignorant or stupid person. It comes from the Sanskrit word for a wilderness. The word jungle has been adopted into English to mean dense or wild forest.

The adjective 'junglee' may have referred, in ancient times, to the people of the forest, the hunter-gatherers who were not familiar with settlements of the plain and with agriculture. It must originally have applied to tribals outside the Hindu caste system.

TIR

My children all have Parsi names. My eldest is called Tamineh, which is not strictly a modern Indian Parsi name but is the contemporary Persian equivalent of Tehmina, the wife of Rustam and mother of Sorab, the legendary heroes of Persian myth. In Persian, the word 'shireen' means sweet. It is used by Parsis (my mother and daughter, for instance) as a female name. The word 'jahan' (another of my daughters) means 'the world', including its wonders. Muslim India uses the word as both a female name, as in Noor Jahan, and a male name, as in Jahangir. Danyal is the Persian-derived name of Akbar's son and deserves to be brought back into popularity with Parsis.

My youngest daughter is called Tir. The English can't pronounce it. They interpose a 'u' sound as though they were saying 'deer' or 'beer'. Then there's the soft 'Th' for 'Tir'. Europeans, at least those who haven't trained in acting school, can't manage it. Poor Tir comes out as 'Tear' and the die-hard hippies who hear it swoon – 'Wow, "tear", that's a far-out name, man!'

If the truth were told, the name came to me in my mother's bathroom, which happened to have a Parsi calendar hanging

on the wall. Practising my faltering Gujarati, I was reading
the names of the days of the month. As a good Zoroastrian
child, I had memorized them, half as well as seven-times-
tables: Hormuz, Bomon, Adibess, Surrevar ... Some of them
I recognized as names. I have a cousin called Bomon and a
sister called Meher. Then I came to the name Tir. I have never
heard it used on a child before, but it passed through me like an
arrow. A strong, unusual and undoubtedly Zoroastrian name.

It had the advantage of being a beautiful 'Indian' idea too:
the Hindi word for an arrow. That was it.

I looked into the derivations. The Persian or Zoroastrian
was ambiguous. One book said that 'Tir' was the name for
Sirius, the Dog Star. I know of it. It's at the bottom of Orion's
Belt. Another book said it was the name for Cupid.

Now that made sense. Cupid? Bow and arrow of love?
Venus's boy? And the word in Hindi meant precisely that –
an arrow, associated now with love, with a merging of Parsi
and Hindu myths and with my daughter. So what if they call
her 'tear' in Britain?

INDEX OF WORDS AND PHRASES